Professional React Admin Development

From Beginner Interface Creation to Advanced Dashboard Optimization and Specialized Backend Integration Techniques

Riley T. Maxwell

Preface

Welcome to **Professional React Admin Development**—a comprehensive guide designed to take you from the basics of React Admin to advanced techniques in building robust, scalable admin dashboards. This book is packed with hands-on examples, expert insights, and practical strategies that will empower you to create sophisticated, user-friendly applications.

In this preface, we'll introduce you to the book's purpose, outline who will benefit most from it, explain how to navigate the content, and clarify the conventions and tools you'll encounter along the way.

About This Book

This book is your complete guide to mastering React Admin—a powerful framework for building dynamic admin dashboards. Whether you're new to React or looking to deepen your expertise, you'll find that this book covers everything from setting up your environment to implementing advanced state management, performance optimization, and secure API integration.

What You'll Learn:

- **Fundamentals and Setup:** Get started with React, create your project, and understand the core components and architecture of React Admin.
- **State Management:** Learn both local and global state management techniques using Hooks, Context API, Redux, and alternatives.
- **Performance Optimization:** Discover strategies to optimize rendering, implement lazy loading, and handle large datasets efficiently.
- **Advanced API Integration:** Dive into building custom data providers for REST and GraphQL, managing asynchronous data, and integrating real-time updates.
- **Security and Authentication:** Implement advanced authentication methods, role-based access control (RBAC), and secure your API endpoints.

- **Data Visualization and Reporting:** Create engaging, interactive, and accessible visualizations to transform raw data into actionable insights.

Personal Insight:
When I first started exploring React Admin, I was overwhelmed by the sheer number of tools and techniques available. This book is a distillation of my experiences—both successes and challenges—aimed at helping you avoid common pitfalls and accelerate your learning journey.

Who Should Read This Book

This book is designed for a wide audience, including:

- **Beginners:** If you're new to React or admin dashboard development, you'll find clear, step-by-step instructions that will help you get started with confidence.
- **Intermediate Developers:** Those with some React experience will benefit from deeper insights into state management, performance optimization, and API integration.
- **Advanced Developers:** Experienced developers looking to explore advanced topics like real-time data integration, custom authentication providers, and scalable architecture.
- **Tech Leads and Architects:** If you're responsible for setting up a robust development framework for your team, this book offers best practices and patterns that ensure maintainable and secure applications.

Personal Insight:
Whether you're a solo developer or part of a larger team, this book is structured to provide value at every level. I've seen how the right knowledge can transform a project's success, and I hope this book becomes a go-to reference in your development toolkit.

How to Use This Book

This book is structured in a modular fashion, allowing you to:

- **Read Sequentially:**
  For a thorough understanding, we recommend starting from the beginning and progressing through each chapter as they build upon one another.
- **Skip to Relevant Sections:**
  If you're already familiar with certain topics, feel free to jump to chapters that cover new or advanced material.
- **Hands-On Practice:**
  Each chapter includes practical code examples and step-by-step instructions. I encourage you to follow along in your development environment to reinforce your learning.
- **Reference Frequently:**
  Use the appendices for quick access to essential resources, debugging tools, and glossary terms.

Personal Insight:
I designed this book to be both a tutorial and a reference guide. My goal is to make it as interactive and practical as possible—so experiment with the examples, take notes, and build your own projects as you learn.

Conventions and Tools

Throughout this book, you'll encounter various conventions and tools that help maintain consistency and clarity:

Code Conventions

- **Syntax Highlighting:**
  Code examples are formatted using standard JavaScript/JSX syntax. Copy and paste the code into your editor to experiment.
- **Comments and Documentation:**
  Each code snippet includes comments explaining key lines and logic. This helps you understand not just how something works, but why it works that way.

Tools and Technologies

- **React and React Admin:**
  The primary frameworks discussed throughout the book.
- **State Management Tools:**
  Including React Hooks, Context API, Redux, and other state management libraries.
- **Chart Libraries:**
  We'll explore Chart.js, Recharts, and D3.js for data visualization.
- **Authentication and Security:**
  Tools like JWT, OAuth, and secure session management techniques are covered in detail.
- **Development Environment:**
  Instructions assume a modern JavaScript development environment with Node.js, npm, and a code editor like Visual Studio Code.

Notation and Terminology

- **Inline Code:**
  Inline code is wrapped in backticks (e.g., `useState`).
- **Block Code:**
  Longer code examples are presented in block format with syntax highlighting.
- **Step-by-Step Instructions:**
  Each practical section provides detailed steps to guide you through the implementation process.

Personal Insight:
Adopting clear conventions and using the right tools can dramatically improve your workflow. Over the years, I've refined my own development process by sticking to consistent practices—this book reflects that approach, aiming to make your learning experience as smooth as possible.

This preface sets the stage for the journey ahead. By understanding the structure of the book, knowing who it's for, and how to use it, you're now equipped to dive into the world of Professional React Admin Development. Whether you're looking to build your first admin dashboard or scale a complex application, the knowledge contained in this book will guide you through every step of the process.

Table of Contents

Part I: Getting Started with React Admin Development

Chapter 1: Introduction to React and React Admin

Welcome to the first chapter of our journey into professional React Admin development! In this chapter, we'll set the stage by exploring how React has evolved to become a cornerstone of modern web development, take a deep dive into what React Admin offers, and compare its advantages with traditional admin solutions. Whether you're new to the React ecosystem or coming from a background in more conventional web development, this chapter is designed to give you a solid understanding of where React stands today and how React Admin can be a game-changer for building efficient, scalable, and engaging admin interfaces.

1.1: The Evolution of React for Modern Web Applications

React has transformed the way we build web interfaces—from its early beginnings as a Facebook experiment to becoming one of the most popular frameworks for creating dynamic, high-performance applications. In this guide, we'll dive into the key milestones of React's evolution, illustrate how these innovations shape modern web development, and provide practical, working code examples along the way.

A Brief History and Key Innovations

Early Days and the Birth of Component-Based Architecture
When React was introduced in 2013, it revolutionized UI development by championing a component-based approach. Instead of building pages as monolithic blocks of code, React broke the UI into small, reusable components. This modular design allowed developers to build, test, and maintain their code more efficiently.

The Virtual DOM – A Game-Changer

One of React's most influential innovations is the Virtual DOM. Rather than updating the browser's Document Object Model (DOM) directly—a process that can be slow and error-prone—React creates a lightweight copy of the DOM. When changes occur, React computes the most efficient way to update the real DOM, significantly enhancing performance and delivering smooth user experiences.

The Introduction of Hooks

For many years, class components were the standard for managing state and lifecycle methods. However, in 2018, React introduced Hooks, which allow developers to use state and other React features in functional components. Hooks simplified the code, improved readability, and reduced the boilerplate associated with class components.

Practical Implementations: Step-by-Step Code Examples

Example 1: A Simple Functional Component

Let's start with a basic functional component. This component renders a greeting message and demonstrates the core idea of component-based architecture.

```
// File: Greeting.js
import React from 'react';

const Greeting = () => {
  return <h1>Hello, welcome to React!</h1>;
};

export default Greeting;
```

How to Use:

You can import and use this component in your main application file. This modular approach enables you to reuse components across your application, making your code more maintainable.

```
// File: App.js
import React from 'react';
```

```
import Greeting from './Greeting';

const App = () => {
  return (
    <div>
      <Greeting />
    </div>
  );
};

export default App;
```

Example 2: Introducing State with Hooks

Now, let's explore a component that uses the useState hook to manage
state. We'll build a simple counter that demonstrates interactive state
updates.

```
// File: Counter.js
import React, { useState } from 'react';

const Counter = () => {
  // Declare a state variable 'count' and a function
'setCount' to update it
  const [count, setCount] = useState(0);

  return (
    <div style={{ textAlign: 'center', marginTop: '2rem'
}}>
      <h2>Counter: {count}</h2>
      <button onClick={() => setCount(count +
1)}>Increase</button>
      <button onClick={() => setCount(count -
1)}>Decrease</button>
    </div>
  );
};

export default Counter;
```

How to Use:
Simply import the Counter component into your application file and
include it within your JSX. This example highlights the simplicity of using
hooks to handle state without the complexities of class components.

```
// File: App.js
import React from 'react';
```

```
import Counter from './Counter';

const App = () => {
  return (
    <div>
      <Counter />
    </div>
  );
};


export default App;
```

Example 3: Using `useEffect` for Side Effects

The `useEffect` hook replaces many of the lifecycle methods from class components. It allows you to perform side effects like data fetching or subscriptions in your functional components. Let's build a component that fetches data from a public API and displays it.

```
// File: DataFetcher.js
import React, { useState, useEffect } from 'react';

const DataFetcher = () => {
  const [data, setData] = useState(null);
  const [loading, setLoading] = useState(true);

  // useEffect runs after the component mounts
  useEffect(() => {
    fetch('https://api.publicapis.org/entries')
      .then((response) => response.json())
      .then((data) => {
        setData(data.entries.slice(0, 5)); // Get first 5
entries for brevity
        setLoading(false);
      })
      .catch((error) => {
        console.error('Error fetching data:', error);
        setLoading(false);
      });
  }, []); // Empty dependency array ensures this runs once
when the component mounts

  if (loading) return <p>Loading data...</p>;

  return (
    <div>
      <h3>Public APIs:</h3>
      <ul>
```

```
      {data.map((entry) => (
        <li key={entry.API}>{entry.Description}</li>
      ))}
    </ul>
  </div>
  );
};

export default DataFetcher;
```

How to Use:

Integrate the `DataFetcher` component into your main application, and it will display live data from the API. This example illustrates how the combination of `useState` and `useEffect` creates powerful, yet simple, asynchronous operations in React.

```
// File: App.js
import React from 'react';
import DataFetcher from './DataFetcher';

const App = () => {
  return (
    <div>
      <DataFetcher />
    </div>
  );
};

export default App;
```

Personal Insights and Expert Commentary

From my experience, React's journey from class-based components to the introduction of Hooks has been nothing short of transformative. Hooks not only simplify your code but also make it more readable and maintainable. This evolution reflects a broader trend in software development: moving toward simplicity and modularity, which allows us to focus on building great user experiences rather than wrestling with boilerplate code.

When I first started with React, understanding the Virtual DOM was a revelation—it explained why React applications could be so much faster than those built with traditional DOM manipulation techniques. Embracing this new way of thinking not only accelerated my development process but also improved the performance of the applications I built.

1.2: Overview of React Admin and Its Ecosystem

React Admin is a powerful framework designed to simplify the creation of admin interfaces and dashboards. Built on top of React, it provides a suite of pre-built components and tools that enable developers to quickly construct fully functional CRUD applications while focusing on business logic instead of repetitive boilerplate code.

In this guide, we'll explore what React Admin is, its key features, and its ecosystem. We'll also walk through a practical, step-by-step implementation of a basic admin dashboard, complete with working code examples and clear documentation.

What Is React Admin?

React Admin is an open-source framework tailored for building admin panels and dashboards. Its design principles revolve around:

- **Component-Based Architecture:**
  React Admin leverages React's component-driven model. This modularity allows you to build, reuse, and customize components easily, leading to more maintainable code.
- **Data-Driven UI:**
  At its core, React Admin is designed to handle CRUD (Create, Read, Update, Delete) operations. It abstracts the complexity of data fetching by integrating with data providers that connect your app to REST, GraphQL, or custom APIs.
- **Built-In Theming and Customization:**
  React Admin is built with Material-UI, ensuring a consistent, modern design. You can easily override styles and components to meet your unique branding and functional requirements.
- **Routing and Authentication:**
  Out-of-the-box, React Admin handles routing and can integrate with custom authentication providers, making it easier to build secure admin interfaces.

Key Components and Architecture

The strength of React Admin lies in its well-organized architecture. Here are the main components you'll work with:

- **`<Admin>` Component:**
  This is the root of your admin application. It sets up the overall layout, routing, and integrates the data provider.
- **`<Resource>` Component:**
  Use this component to declare different data resources (e.g., posts, users). Each resource is typically associated with views for listing, editing, creating, and showing details.
- **CRUD Views:**
  React Admin provides pre-built views such as `<List>`, `<Create>`, `<Edit>`, and `<Show>` that allow you to quickly implement standard CRUD operations.
- **Data Provider:**
  This function maps your application's data operations (like GET, POST, PUT, DELETE) to the API endpoints. There are several pre-made data providers available (e.g., `ra-data-json-server`), which make connecting to popular backends straightforward.

Practical Implementation: A Step-by-Step Guide

Let's build a simple admin dashboard that displays a list of posts using a public API. This practical example will show you how to set up React Admin from scratch.

Step 1: Set Up Your Project

Start by creating a new React application (if you haven't already) and installing React Admin along with a JSON server data provider:

```
npx create-react-app react-admin-demo
cd react-admin-demo
```

```
npm install react-admin ra-data-json-server
```

Step 2: Create the Admin Application

Create an `App.js` file (or modify your existing one) to set up the admin interface. In this example, we will fetch posts from the JSONPlaceholder API.

```
// File: App.js
import React from 'react';
import { Admin, Resource, List, Datagrid, TextField } from
'react-admin';
import jsonServerProvider from 'ra-data-json-server';

// Set up the data provider pointing to the JSONPlaceholder
API
const dataProvider =
jsonServerProvider('https://jsonplaceholder.typicode.com');

// Define a List view for posts
const PostList = () => (
  <List>
    <Datagrid rowClick="edit">
      <TextField source="id" label="ID" />
      <TextField source="title" label="Title" />
      <TextField source="body" label="Content" />
    </Datagrid>
  </List>
);

// Main App component integrating React Admin
const App = () => (
  <Admin dataProvider={dataProvider}>
    <Resource name="posts" list={PostList} />
  </Admin>
);

export default App;
```

Step 3: Run Your Application

After saving your changes, start your development server:

```
npm start
```

Your browser should open a basic admin interface listing posts from the JSONPlaceholder API. This example demonstrates the ease of integrating a data provider and using built-in components to quickly generate a functional admin dashboard.

The Ecosystem Around React Admin

React Admin is supported by a vibrant community and a robust ecosystem. Here are some of the benefits and resources available:

- **Custom Components & Extensions:**
  You can easily override or extend default components. This means if you need a custom behavior or design, you can build your own component and integrate it seamlessly.
- **Authentication & Authorization:**
  Secure your admin interface with custom authentication providers. React Admin supports various methods (JWT, OAuth, etc.) to manage user sessions and permissions.
- **Third-Party Plugins:**
  The ecosystem includes plugins and libraries for additional functionalities, such as charts and data visualizations, which can be integrated to enhance your admin dashboards.
- **Comprehensive Documentation & Community Support:**
  With extensive documentation and an active community, troubleshooting and expanding your application is simpler. The community frequently shares insights, plugins, and best practices that further enhance the development process.

When I first explored React Admin, I was pleasantly surprised by how quickly I could set up a fully functional admin dashboard. The framework's modular design and pre-built components drastically reduced development time and allowed me to focus on creating a unique user experience. Over time, I've come to appreciate its flexibility and the way it seamlessly integrates with modern backends. Whether you're building a small project or a large-scale enterprise solution, React Admin provides a robust foundation that can evolve with your needs.

1.3: Comparing React Admin with Traditional Admin Solutions

When building admin interfaces, developers have two primary options: leveraging modern frameworks like React Admin or using traditional admin solutions that often rely on older technologies. In this guide, we'll explore the strengths and weaknesses of both approaches, backed by practical code examples to illustrate how each method works in a real-world scenario.

The Traditional Approach: Overview and Practical Example

Traditional admin solutions are often built with server-side languages like PHP, ASP.NET, or even plain JavaScript/jQuery. These solutions typically follow a monolithic architecture, where the UI is tightly coupled with the backend. Here are some key characteristics:

- **Monolithic Architecture:**
  Traditional solutions generally handle both the frontend and backend in a single, tightly integrated codebase. This can make scaling and maintenance more challenging over time.
- **Manual DOM Manipulation:**
  Tools like jQuery were once the go-to for dynamic UI updates. However, updating the DOM manually means developers must manage performance, state synchronization, and potential bugs.
- **Limited Reusability:**
  With a traditional approach, UI components tend to be less modular and reusable, leading to more duplicated code and slower development cycles.
- **Server-Side Rendering:**
  Many traditional admin panels rely on server-side rendering. While this can benefit SEO and initial load times, it may result in less responsive interfaces once the application is running.

Traditional Admin Example: A Simple Dashboard with jQuery

Below is a minimal example that demonstrates a traditional approach using HTML, CSS, and jQuery to build a dashboard that fetches and displays a list of posts.

Step 1: Set Up the HTML Structure

Create a file called `index.html`:

```html
<!DOCTYPE html>
<html lang="en">
<head>
  <meta charset="UTF-8" />
  <title>Traditional Admin Dashboard</title>
  <style>
    body { font-family: Arial, sans-serif; margin: 20px; }
    table { width: 100%; border-collapse: collapse; margin-top: 20px; }
    th, td { border: 1px solid #ccc; padding: 8px; text-align: left; }
    th { background-color: #f4f4f4; }
  </style>
</head>
<body>
  <h1>Admin Dashboard</h1>
  <table id="postsTable">
    <thead>
      <tr>
        <th>ID</th>
        <th>Title</th>
      </tr>
    </thead>
    <tbody>
      <!-- Data will be injected here -->
    </tbody>
  </table>

  <!-- Include jQuery from a CDN -->
  <script src="https://code.jquery.com/jquery-3.6.0.min.js"></script>
  <script src="app.js"></script>
</body>
</html>
```

Step 2: Write jQuery Code to Fetch and Display Data

Create a file called `app.js`:

```js
$(document).ready(function () {
```

```
// Use a public API for demonstration purposes
$.ajax({
  url: 'https://jsonplaceholder.typicode.com/posts',
  method: 'GET',
  success: function (data) {
    const tbody = $('#postsTable tbody');
    // For brevity, only show the first 5 posts
    data.slice(0, 5).forEach(post => {
      const row = `<tr>
                     <td>${post.id}</td>
                     <td>${post.title}</td>
                   </tr>`;
      tbody.append(row);
    });
  },
  error: function () {
    alert('Failed to load data.');
  }
});
});
```

How It Works:

- The HTML file provides a basic structure with a table.
- jQuery's `$.ajax` function fetches post data from a public API.
- The data is then manually appended to the table's `<tbody>`.

Pros of the Traditional Approach:

- Quick setup for small, straightforward applications.
- Direct control over every DOM element.

Cons:

- Manual DOM manipulation can lead to code that's hard to maintain.
- Scaling and adding complex features often result in tangled code and performance bottlenecks.

The React Admin Approach: Overview and Practical Example

React Admin, built on top of React, introduces a modern, component-driven methodology that emphasizes modularity, reusability, and performance. Key features include:

- **Component-Based Architecture:**
  React Admin breaks down the UI into small, reusable components, making your codebase more modular and easier to maintain.
- **Declarative Data Fetching:**
  With built-in data providers, React Admin abstracts the complexity of data operations. CRUD functionalities are available out-of-the-box.
- **Built-In Routing and Theming:**
  The framework handles routing, theming, and many common admin tasks, allowing you to focus on business logic.
- **Scalability:**
  React Admin is designed to handle complex, data-driven interfaces with ease, using modern practices like lazy loading and virtualized lists.

React Admin Example: A Simple Dashboard Listing Posts

Below is a step-by-step implementation of a similar dashboard using React Admin.

Step 1: Set Up the React Project

Create a new React project and install React Admin:

```
npx create-react-app react-admin-demo
cd react-admin-demo
npm install react-admin ra-data-json-server
```

Step 2: Build the Admin Dashboard

Edit the `App.js` file with the following code:

```
// File: App.js
import React from 'react';
import { Admin, Resource, List, Datagrid, TextField } from
'react-admin';
import jsonServerProvider from 'ra-data-json-server';

// Define the data provider for the JSONPlaceholder API
```

```
const dataProvider =
jsonServerProvider('https://jsonplaceholder.typicode.com');

// Define the list view for posts
const PostList = () => (
  <List>
    <Datagrid rowClick="edit">
      <TextField source="id" label="ID" />
      <TextField source="title" label="Title" />
    </Datagrid>
  </List>
);

// Main App component integrating React Admin
const App = () => (
  <Admin dataProvider={dataProvider}>
    <Resource name="posts" list={PostList} />
  </Admin>
);

export default App;
```

How It Works:

- The `<Admin>` component initializes the admin interface, integrating the data provider seamlessly.
- `<Resource>` defines the data model, and `<List>` with `<Datagrid>` automatically handles the rendering of data in a table format.

Pros of the React Admin Approach:

- **Efficiency:** Rapid development with pre-built components for common tasks.
- **Maintainability:** A modular structure that makes it easier to manage and scale your application.
- **Customization:** Built-in theming and customization options let you tailor the interface to your needs.

Cons:

- A learning curve exists for developers unfamiliar with React and modern JavaScript patterns.
- The abstraction might feel limiting if you need very fine-grained control over every UI detail (though it's highly extensible).

Personal Insights and Expert Commentary

In my own projects, switching from traditional admin solutions to React Admin has been a turning point. The reduction in boilerplate code and the emphasis on reusable components has not only sped up development but also made the codebase easier to maintain. Instead of juggling multiple scripts and manual DOM updates, React Admin lets you focus on building features that matter.

While traditional solutions might suffice for simple applications, they often struggle with complexity and scalability. React Admin's design philosophy—centered around modern web practices like declarative programming and component modularity—proves to be a game-changer, especially for projects that need to grow and evolve over time.

Chapter 2: Setting Up the Development Environment

In this chapter, we'll lay the foundation for your React Admin journey by setting up your development environment. Whether you're a beginner or coming from a different tech stack, this step-by-step guide will ensure you have everything you need to start building modern admin interfaces. We'll cover installing essential tools, bootstrapping a React project, installing React Admin, and understanding the project structure.

2.1: Installing Node.js, npm, and Essential Tools

Before you dive into building your React Admin application, it's essential to set up a robust development environment. This section covers how to install Node.js and npm—two foundational tools for modern JavaScript development—as well as other essential utilities like a code editor and Git. We'll walk through each step with clear explanations, practical commands, and personal insights to help you get started smoothly.

Why Node.js and npm?

Node.js is a JavaScript runtime built on Chrome's V8 engine that lets you run JavaScript outside the browser. It's essential for server-side development and running build tools for your React projects. **npm** (Node Package Manager) comes bundled with Node.js and is your gateway to thousands of packages and libraries that can simplify your development process.

Personal Insight:
When I first started with web development, setting up Node.js and npm was a transformative step. It opened the door to using modern tools and

libraries, streamlining my workflow and allowing me to focus on building great applications rather than wrestling with configuration issues.

Step 1: Downloading and Installing Node.js and npm

For Windows and macOS Users:

1. **Visit the Official Website:**
   Open your browser and navigate to nodejs.org.
2. **Choose the LTS Version:**
   The Long Term Support (LTS) version is recommended for most users because it offers stability and long-term maintenance. Click the download link for your operating system.
3. **Run the Installer:**
   Follow the installer prompts:
   - **Windows:** Run the `.msi` installer and follow the setup wizard.
   - **macOS:** Open the `.pkg` file and follow the installation instructions.

For Linux Users:

If you're on Linux, you can install Node.js using your distribution's package manager. For example, on Ubuntu:

```
# Update your package index
sudo apt update

# Install Node.js and npm
sudo apt install nodejs npm
```

Alternative for Linux and macOS:
Using Node Version Manager (nvm) is highly recommended if you need to manage multiple Node.js versions. To install nvm, run:

```
curl -o- https://raw.githubusercontent.com/nvm-sh/nvm/v0.39.4/install.sh | bash
```

Then, install the latest LTS version:

```
nvm install --lts
```

Step 2: Verifying the Installation

After installing Node.js and npm, verify that the installation was successful by opening your terminal (or Command Prompt on Windows) and running:

```
node -v
npm -v
```

These commands should print the version numbers of Node.js and npm respectively. For example, you might see something like:

```
v16.15.0
8.5.5
```

This confirms that both tools are correctly installed and ready to use.

Step 3: Installing Essential Tools

1. Visual Studio Code (VSCode)

A great code editor is vital for efficient development. **VSCode** is highly popular due to its robust ecosystem, integrated terminal, and extensive plugin library.

- **Download VSCode:**
  Visit code.visualstudio.com and download the installer for your OS.
- **Install Recommended Extensions:**
  Some useful extensions for React development include:
    - **ESLint:** for code linting
    - **Prettier:** for code formatting
    - **Bracket Pair Colorizer:** for easier code navigation

2. Git

Git is essential for version control and collaboration.

- **Download Git:**
  Visit git-scm.com and follow the installation instructions.
- **Configure Git:**
  After installation, open your terminal and run the following commands to set your identity:

```
git config --global user.name "Your Name"
git config --global user.email "you@example.com"
```

Personal Insight:
I found that a well-configured Git setup not only improves my workflow but also makes it easier to collaborate on projects and track changes effectively.

2.2: Bootstrapping with Create React App

One of the most exciting parts of starting a new React project is bootstrapping it with a tool that handles all the heavy lifting for you. Create React App (CRA) is the industry-standard tool for quickly setting up a modern React development environment with zero configuration. In this guide, we'll walk through how to use CRA step by step, explain what happens behind the scenes, and share some personal insights on making the most of it.

What Is Create React App?

Create React App is an officially supported tool that generates a fully functional React project with a preconfigured build setup. It handles the setup of tools like Babel, Webpack, and a development server, so you don't have to worry about configuring them manually. This allows you to focus on writing your application code rather than spending time on build configuration.

Personal Insight:
I remember the relief I felt the first time I ran CRA—instantly, I could see the power of React without the hassle of configuration. It gave me the freedom to dive straight into building components and features, knowing that the environment was already optimized for development.

Step-by-Step Guide to Bootstrapping Your React Project

Step 1: Open Your Terminal

Open your preferred terminal or command prompt. Make sure you are in the directory where you want your new project to live.

Step 2: Create a New React Application

Run the following command to create a new React project. Replace `my-admin-app` with your desired project name.

```
npx create-react-app my-admin-app
```

What Happens Here:

- **npx:** A tool that comes with npm and lets you run commands from npm packages without installing them globally.
- **create-react-app:** The package that sets up your new React project.
- **my-admin-app:** The directory name for your new project.

This command downloads the latest version of Create React App, sets up the project structure, installs dependencies, and creates a boilerplate codebase for you.

Step 3: Navigate into Your Project Directory

Once the command completes, move into your project folder:

```
cd my-admin-app
```

Step 4: Start the Development Server

To see your new React application in action, start the development server with:

```
npm start
```

This command does a few things:

- It compiles your application.
- It opens your default browser to http://localhost:3000.
- It sets up a live-reloading development environment, so any changes you make in your code will automatically refresh in the browser.

Personal Insight:
The moment the browser opened and displayed the default React page, I knew I was ready to build something amazing. The immediate feedback provided by the live-reload feature has been invaluable during development—it saves time and helps catch issues early.

Exploring the Generated Project Structure

After bootstrapping your project, you'll notice a well-organized structure. Here's a quick overview of the key files and directories:

- **public/ Directory:**
  Contains the index.html file, which is the entry point of your web application. You might add static assets like images or fonts here.
- **src/ Directory:**
  This is where all your React components and application logic live. Key files include:
  - **index.js:** The JavaScript entry point that renders your React application into the DOM.
  - **App.js:** The main component where you can start building your application.
  - **App.css:** The default styling for your application.
- **package.json:**
  Lists your project dependencies, scripts, and metadata. This file is

essential for managing your project's configuration and dependencies.

Understanding this structure early on helps you keep your code organized as your project grows.

Practical Example: Modifying the App Component

Let's make a small change to see how the live-reloading works. Open src/App.js in your code editor and modify it as follows:

```
// File: src/App.js
import React from 'react';
import './App.css';

function App() {
  return (
    <div className="App">
      <header className="App-header">
        <h1>Welcome to My Admin App!</h1>
        <p>This is your starting point for building a
powerful admin interface.</p>
      </header>
    </div>
  );
}

export default App;
```

Save the file, and watch as your browser automatically updates with the new message. This quick feedback loop makes it easy to experiment and iterate on your design.

2.3: Installing and Configuring React Admin

Once you've bootstrapped your React project with Create React App, the next exciting step is integrating React Admin into your application. React Admin is designed to simplify the creation of robust admin interfaces, providing pre-built components and a powerful data management layer. In this guide, we'll walk through installing React Admin, configuring it, and setting up a simple example to get you started.

Why React Admin?

React Admin takes the heavy lifting out of building admin dashboards by offering:

- **Pre-built CRUD components:** Quickly set up lists, forms, and detail views.
- **Flexible Data Providers:** Easily connect to REST APIs, GraphQL, or custom backends.
- **Theming and Customization:** Leverage Material-UI for a modern look, with the ability to override and extend components.
- **Built-in Routing and Authentication:** Simplify navigation and secure your admin panels.

Personal Insight:
When I first integrated React Admin into a project, the reduction in boilerplate code was immediately apparent. I could focus on delivering business features without worrying about routine CRUD operations and state management nuances.

Step-by-Step Installation and Configuration

Step 1: Install React Admin and a Data Provider

Open your terminal in your project directory and run the following command:

```
npm install react-admin ra-data-json-server
```

- **react-admin:** The core library for building your admin interface.
- **ra-data-json-server:** A data provider that works seamlessly with REST APIs like JSONPlaceholder, perfect for demos and quick prototyping.

Step 2: Set Up Your Main Admin Component

Next, you'll configure your admin interface. Open your `src/App.js` file and replace its contents with the following code:

```
// File: src/App.js
import React from 'react';
import { Admin, Resource, List, Datagrid, TextField } from
'react-admin';
import jsonServerProvider from 'ra-data-json-server';

// Step 2.1: Configure the Data Provider
// This connects React Admin to a demo API endpoint.
const dataProvider =
jsonServerProvider('https://jsonplaceholder.typicode.com');

// Step 2.2: Define a Simple List View for 'posts'
const PostList = () => (
  <List>
    <Datagrid rowClick="edit">
      <TextField source="id" label="ID" />
      <TextField source="title" label="Title" />
      <TextField source="body" label="Body" />
    </Datagrid>
  </List>
);

// Step 2.3: Configure the Admin Component with a Resource
const App = () => (
  <Admin dataProvider={dataProvider}>
    <Resource name="posts" list={PostList} />
  </Admin>
);

export default App;
```

Explanation:

- **Data Provider:**
  The `jsonServerProvider` function creates a bridge between your React Admin app and the REST API at `https://jsonplaceholder.typicode.com`. This API is a common demo resource that returns posts, comments, and more.
- **List Component:**
  The `PostList` component uses React Admin's `<List>` and `<Datagrid>` components to render a table of posts. The `rowClick="edit"` property indicates that clicking a row should navigate to an edit view (which you can implement later).
- **Resource Registration:**
  The `<Resource>` component registers the `posts` resource with your admin interface. React Admin automatically generates routes and hooks into the data provider for CRUD operations.

Personal Insight:
Integrating React Admin was as simple as adding a few lines of code. The framework's structure allowed me to see results almost immediately. This rapid feedback loop is crucial when you're iterating on features and exploring new functionalities.

Step 3: Run and Test Your Application

Now that everything is set up, start your development server:

```
npm start
```

Your browser should automatically open at `http://localhost:3000`, displaying your new admin interface. You should see a table listing posts fetched from the JSONPlaceholder API. If everything looks good, congratulations—you've successfully installed and configured React Admin!

Tips for Further Configuration

Customizing Components

- **Theming:**
  React Admin uses Material-UI, so you can customize the look and

feel by overriding default themes. Explore Material-UI's theming documentation to tailor the design to your needs.

- **Extending CRUD Views:**
  While the example above uses basic list views, React Admin supports custom create, edit, and show views. You can build your own components or extend the built-in ones to include more complex interactions.

Adding Authentication and Routing

- **Authentication:**
  For secure admin applications, consider integrating custom authentication providers. React Admin supports various methods, such as JWT or OAuth.
- **Custom Routes:**
  If you need non-standard pages or additional functionality, you can define custom routes within the `<Admin>` component.

2.4: Understanding the Project Structure

When you first create a React project—especially one enhanced with React Admin—it might feel overwhelming to navigate the various folders and files. However, understanding the project structure early on is key to maintaining clarity and scalability as your application grows. In this guide, we'll break down the essential parts of your project, explain their roles, and offer practical tips on organizing your code effectively.

Overview of the Default Structure

After bootstrapping your project with Create React App, you'll notice a clean and organized structure. Here's a typical layout:

```
my-admin-app/
├── node_modules/
├── public/
│   ├── index.html
│   └── ... (other static assets)
├── src/
```

```
            ├── App.css
            ├── App.js
            ├── index.css
            ├── index.js
            └── ... (other components, utilities, etc.)
    ├── .gitignore
    ├── package.json
    └── README.md
```

Each part of this structure has a specific role:

- **node_modules/**:
  Contains all third-party libraries installed via npm. You don't need to modify these files directly.
- **public/**:
  Holds static assets like `index.html`, which serves as the entry point of your application. You might also place images, fonts, or icons here.
  Example: The `index.html` file includes a `<div id="root"></div>`, which is where your React app is injected.
- **src/**:
  This is the heart of your application. All of your React components, styles, and business logic reside here.
    - **index.js:**
      The JavaScript entry point that renders your React application into the DOM.

```
// File: src/index.js
import React from 'react';
import ReactDOM from 'react-dom';
import './index.css';
import App from './App';

ReactDOM.render(
  <React.StrictMode>
    <App />
  </React.StrictMode>,
  document.getElementById('root')
);
```

    - **App.js:**
      The main component where you set up routes, integrate React Admin, or compose your application's overall layout.

```
// File: src/App.js
```

```
import React from 'react';
import { Admin, Resource, List, Datagrid, TextField } from
'react-admin';
import jsonServerProvider from 'ra-data-json-server';

const dataProvider =
jsonServerProvider('https://jsonplaceholder.typicode.com');
const PostList = () => (
  <List>
    <Datagrid rowClick="edit">
      <TextField source="id" label="ID" />
      <TextField source="title" label="Title" />
      <TextField source="body" label="Body" />
    </Datagrid>
  </List>
);

const App = () => (
  <Admin dataProvider={dataProvider}>
    <Resource name="posts" list={PostList} />
  </Admin>
);

export default App;
```

- **package.json:**
  Contains metadata about your project and a list of all
  dependencies. It also defines useful scripts, like `npm start` for
  running the development server or `npm run build` for production.

Organizing Your Code as Your Project Grows

While the default structure is perfect for getting started, you'll likely want
to reorganize as your application becomes more complex. Here are some
best practices:

1. Create a Components Directory

Instead of placing all components directly in `src/`, create a folder for
reusable components.

```
src/
├── components/
│   ├── Header.js
```

```
│   ├── Footer.js
│   └── CustomButton.js
└── ...
```

2. Separate Views or Pages

For an admin dashboard, you might have distinct pages or views. Create a directory for these, which can include components for listing data, editing forms, etc.

```
src/
├── pages/
│   ├── Dashboard.js
│   ├── PostList.js
│   └── PostEdit.js
└── ...
```

3. Group Related Files

You might also group files by feature. For example, if you have several components related to "posts", create a folder for them:

```
src/
├── posts/
│   ├── PostList.js
│   ├── PostEdit.js
│   └── postService.js
└── ...
```

4. Maintain a Clean Public Directory

Keep the `public/` folder reserved for static assets that won't be processed by Webpack. This ensures your build remains optimized.

Personal Insights on Project Organization

When I first started building with React Admin, I was amazed at how clean the default structure was. However, as the application evolved, adopting a modular structure (by separating components, pages, and services) made it far easier to manage and scale. Investing time in setting up a thoughtful directory structure early on pays dividends later, as it minimizes refactoring and makes onboarding new team members more straightforward.

For instance, by placing all post-related components in a dedicated folder, I could quickly locate and update features without digging through a monolithic `src/` directory. It's all about creating a system that suits your workflow and project needs.

Understanding the project structure is more than just knowing where files live—it's about organizing your code in a way that promotes clarity, scalability, and maintainability. The default structure provided by Create React App gives you a strong starting point, and with some thoughtful adjustments, you can create an environment that supports efficient development and collaboration.

Take the time to review and adjust your project layout as needed. With a well-organized structure, you'll find it easier to manage complexity and build high-quality admin interfaces with React Admin.

Chapter 3: Fundamentals of React Components and Architecture

In this chapter, we delve into the core building blocks of React—components. You'll learn about functional components and Hooks, explore the powerful combination of JSX, props, and state, discover techniques for composing reusable components, and review various styling approaches including CSS, CSS-in-JS, and Material-UI. This foundation will empower you to build dynamic, scalable, and maintainable applications.

3.1: Functional Components and Hooks

Functional components and Hooks form the backbone of modern React development. In this section, we'll explore what functional components are, why they're favored over class components, and how Hooks empower these components to manage state and side effects. We'll break down each concept step by step, provide working code examples, and share practical insights along the way.

What Are Functional Components?

Functional components are simply JavaScript functions that return JSX (React's syntax extension for HTML). They are clean, concise, and focus solely on rendering UI based on input properties. Unlike class components, functional components are easier to write and understand because they avoid the complexity of lifecycle methods and `this` binding.

A Simple Functional Component

Let's start with a basic example:

```
// File: src/components/Greeting.js
```

```
import React from 'react';

const Greeting = () => {
  return <h1>Hello, welcome to React!</h1>;
};

export default Greeting;
```

Explanation:

- The `Greeting` component is a plain function that returns a heading element.
- It uses no internal state or lifecycle methods, making it very straightforward.

Personal Insight:
I found that switching to functional components simplified my codebase significantly. They are much easier to test and reason about because each component is just a function with predictable output.

Introducing Hooks

Hooks revolutionized functional components by allowing them to manage state and side effects—capabilities that were previously exclusive to class components. The two most commonly used Hooks are `useState` and `useEffect`.

useState: Managing Local State

The `useState` Hook lets you add state to your functional components. Here's a step-by-step example of a counter component:

```
// File: src/components/Counter.js
import React, { useState } from 'react';

const Counter = () => {
  // Declare a state variable 'count' and a function
'setCount' to update it.
  const [count, setCount] = useState(0);

  return (
```

```
    <div style={{ textAlign: 'center', marginTop: '2rem'
}}>
      <h2>Counter: {count}</h2>
      <button onClick={() => setCount(count +
1)}>Increase</button>
      <button onClick={() => setCount(count -
1)}>Decrease</button>
    </div>
  );
};

export default Counter;
```

Step-by-Step Breakdown:

1. **Import useState:**
   We import `useState` from React.
2. **Declare State:**
   The line `const [count, setCount] = useState(0);` initializes
   a state variable `count` with an initial value of `0`. The `setCount`
   function is used to update this state.
3. **Render UI:**
   The component returns JSX that displays the current count and
   includes buttons to increment or decrement it.

Personal Insight:
The clarity and simplicity of `useState` made it easy for me to handle
dynamic data in my components without the overhead of classes. It
encourages a more functional programming style, which aligns well with
modern JavaScript practices.

useEffect: Handling Side Effects

The `useEffect` Hook lets you perform side effects in functional
components. It replaces several lifecycle methods like
`componentDidMount`, `componentDidUpdate`, and
`componentWillUnmount` found in class components.

Example: Fetching Data on Component Mount

Here's a practical example where we fetch data from an API when the
component mounts:

```
// File: src/components/DataFetcher.js
import React, { useState, useEffect } from 'react';

const DataFetcher = () => {
  const [data, setData] = useState([]);
  const [loading, setLoading] = useState(true);

  // useEffect runs after the component mounts.
  useEffect(() => {
    fetch('https://jsonplaceholder.typicode.com/posts')
      .then((response) => response.json())
      .then((data) => {
        setData(data.slice(0, 5)); // Display first 5 posts
for brevity.
        setLoading(false);
      })
      .catch((error) => {
        console.error('Error fetching data:', error);
        setLoading(false);
      });
  }, []); // The empty dependency array ensures this effect
runs only once.

  if (loading) return <p>Loading data...</p>;

  return (
    <div>
      <h3>Fetched Posts:</h3>
      <ul>
        {data.map((post) => (
          <li key={post.id}>{post.title}</li>
        ))}
      </ul>
    </div>
  );
};

export default DataFetcher;
```

Step-by-Step Breakdown:

1. **Initialize State:**
   We use useState to declare data (an array to store posts) and loading (a boolean to indicate loading status).
2. **Set Up useEffect:**
   The useEffect hook is used to fetch data from an API when the component mounts. The empty dependency array [] means the effect runs only once.

3. **Handle Data:**
   Once data is fetched, we update the state with the first five posts and set `loading` to `false`.
4. **Conditional Rendering:**
   While data is being fetched, the component renders a "Loading data..." message.

Personal Insight:
Using `useEffect` for data fetching drastically reduced the complexity compared to managing similar logic in class components. It neatly encapsulated the side effect, making the component easier to read and maintain.

3.2: JSX, Props, and State

Understanding JSX, props, and state is fundamental to working with React. These three concepts are the building blocks that allow you to build dynamic, reusable, and interactive user interfaces. In this guide, we'll break down each concept, explain how they work together, and provide clear, step-by-step code examples.

What is JSX?

JSX stands for JavaScript XML. It is a syntax extension for JavaScript that lets you write HTML-like code within your JavaScript files. While it looks similar to HTML, JSX is transformed into standard JavaScript that creates React elements.

Key Points About JSX:

- **Declarative Syntax:**
  JSX allows you to describe what your UI should look like in a clear and declarative way.
- **Embedded JavaScript:**
  You can embed JavaScript expressions inside JSX using curly braces `{}`.

- **Compilation:**
  Under the hood, JSX is compiled by tools like Babel into `React.createElement` calls.

Example: A Simple JSX Component

```js
// File: src/components/SimpleMessage.js
import React from 'react';

const SimpleMessage = () => {
  const name = "World";
  return (
    <div>
      <h1>Hello, {name}!</h1>
      <p>This is an example of JSX in action.</p>
    </div>
  );
};

export default SimpleMessage;
```

Explanation:

- We declare a variable `name` and embed it within an `<h1>` tag.
- The JSX syntax closely resembles HTML, making it intuitive and easy to understand.

Personal Insight:
I remember how intuitive JSX felt when I first encountered it. Its clear syntax allowed me to visualize the UI directly within the code, bridging the gap between design and logic.

Understanding Props

Props (short for properties) are how you pass data from a parent component to a child component. They make your components flexible and reusable.

Key Points About Props:

- **Immutable:**
  Props are read-only. Once passed to a component, they should not be modified.
- **Data Flow:**
  They enable a unidirectional data flow, which means data moves from parent to child.
- **Customization:**
  With props, you can customize components with dynamic data.

Example: Passing Props to a Component

```
// File: src/components/UserProfile.js
import React from 'react';

const UserProfile = ({ name, bio }) => {
  return (
    <div className="user-profile">
      <h2>{name}</h2>
      <p>{bio}</p>
    </div>
  );
};

export default UserProfile;
```

And using this component in another file:

```
// File: src/App.js
import React from 'react';
import UserProfile from './components/UserProfile';

const App = () => {
  return (
    <div>
      <UserProfile name="Alice Johnson" bio="Frontend
Developer and React enthusiast." />
      <UserProfile name="Bob Smith" bio="Full-stack
Developer with a passion for clean code." />
    </div>
  );
};

export default App;
```

Explanation:

- The `UserProfile` component receives `name` and `bio` as props.
- The parent component (`App`) passes different values for each instance of `UserProfile`.

Personal Insight:
Using props transformed how I built interfaces. It allowed me to create generic components that could be easily reused and configured with different data, making my code much more modular and maintainable.

Understanding State

State represents data that can change over time within a component. Unlike props, state is managed within the component and can be updated based on user interactions or other events.

Key Points About State:

- **Local and Mutable:**
  State is local to a component and can be updated using state management functions like `setState` (in class components) or the `useState` Hook (in functional components).
- **Triggers Re-render:**
  When state changes, React re-renders the component to reflect the updated data.
- **Encapsulation:**
  State is encapsulated within the component, making it independent of other parts of the application.

Example: Managing State with useState

```
// File: src/components/InteractiveCounter.js
import React, { useState } from 'react';

const InteractiveCounter = () => {
  // Declare a state variable 'count' and a function
'setCount' to update it.
  const [count, setCount] = useState(0);

  return (
    <div style={{ textAlign: 'center', marginTop: '2rem'
}}>
```

```
      <h2>Current Count: {count}</h2>
      <button onClick={() => setCount(count +
1)}>Increase</button>
      <button onClick={() => setCount(count -
1)}>Decrease</button>
    </div>
  );
};

export default InteractiveCounter;
```

Explanation:

- We initialize a state variable `count` with an initial value of `0` using `useState`.
- The `setCount` function is used to update the state.
- When the state changes, the component re-renders, showing the updated count.

Personal Insight:

I've always appreciated how state management with Hooks like `useState` makes handling dynamic data so intuitive. It removes much of the complexity that came with class-based components and lifecycle methods, allowing for a more streamlined development process.

Bringing It All Together

To see JSX, props, and state working in harmony, let's create a small interactive component that displays a personalized greeting and allows the user to update a message.

Example: Personalized Greeting with Dynamic Message

```
// File: src/components/PersonalizedGreeting.js
import React, { useState } from 'react';

const PersonalizedGreeting = ({ initialName }) => {
  // State for the message and user input
  const [message, setMessage] = useState('Welcome to our
application!');
  const [input, setInput] = useState('');
```

```
  const updateMessage = () => {
    setMessage(input);
    setInput(''); // Clear input after updating
  };

  return (
    <div style={{ padding: '1rem', border: '1px solid
#ccc', borderRadius: '8px' }}>
      <h2>Hello, {initialName}!</h2>
      <p>{message}</p>
      <input
        type="text"
        placeholder="Type a new message"
        value={input}
        onChange={(e) => setInput(e.target.value)}
        style={{ padding: '0.5rem', width: '70%',
marginRight: '0.5rem' }}
      />
      <button onClick={updateMessage} style={{ padding:
'0.5rem 1rem' }}>
        Update Message
      </button>
    </div>
  );
};

export default PersonalizedGreeting;
```

And use this component in your main app:

```
// File: src/App.js
import React from 'react';
import PersonalizedGreeting from
'./components/PersonalizedGreeting';

const App = () => {
  return (
    <div>
      <PersonalizedGreeting initialName="Alex" />
    </div>
  );
};

export default App;
```

Explanation:

- The `PersonalizedGreeting` component receives `initialName` as a prop.
- It uses state to manage both a custom message and the user's input.
- Users can type a new message, and upon clicking the button, the state updates and the UI reflects the new message immediately.

Personal Insight:
This example demonstrates the power of combining JSX, props, and state. It not only makes the UI dynamic and interactive but also provides a clear structure for managing data flow within the component. This approach has consistently helped me build components that are both engaging and easy to maintain.

3.3: Component Composition and Reusability

One of React's greatest strengths is its ability to break down a user interface into small, manageable pieces. Component composition and reusability are key principles that enable you to build scalable and maintainable applications. In this guide, we'll explore how to structure your components to maximize reuse and simplify your codebase. We'll dive into practical examples and provide step-by-step explanations along the way.

Why Component Composition Matters

Component composition is the process of combining simple components to build more complex UIs. Instead of writing one large component, you split functionality into smaller, self-contained pieces that can be easily reused across your application.

Benefits include:

- **Maintainability:** Smaller components are easier to update and debug.

- **Reusability:** Common functionality can be packaged once and used in multiple places.
- **Testability:** Isolated components are simpler to test individually.
- **Readability:** A well-composed UI is more understandable because each component has a single responsibility.

Personal Insight:
I've found that once I started breaking down my UI into smaller components, my development process became more agile. Debugging was less of a headache, and I could reuse components in multiple projects, saving a lot of time.

Building a Reusable Component: The Reusable Button

Let's start by creating a simple, reusable button component. This button can accept props like `label`, `onClick`, and even a custom style to adapt to various parts of your application.

```
// File: src/components/CustomButton.js
import React from 'react';
import PropTypes from 'prop-types';

const CustomButton = ({ label, onClick, style }) => {
  return (
    <button onClick={onClick} style={{ padding: '0.5rem
1rem', ...style }}>
      {label}
    </button>
  );
};

CustomButton.propTypes = {
  label: PropTypes.string.isRequired,
  onClick: PropTypes.func,
  style: PropTypes.object,
};

CustomButton.defaultProps = {
  onClick: () => {},
  style: {},
};
```

```
export default CustomButton;
```

Explanation:

- **Props:**
  `label` displays text, `onClick` handles user interactions, and `style` allows custom styling.
- **Default Props & PropTypes:**
  Ensuring the component is robust and its API is clear.

This component can now be reused anywhere you need a button with similar behavior.

Composing a Complex UI: A Dashboard Example

Imagine you're building an admin dashboard. You can create separate components for the header, sidebar, content area, and footer, then compose them into one cohesive layout.

Step 1: Define the Header Component

```
// File: src/components/Header.js
import React from 'react';

const Header = () => (
  <header style={{ background: '#282c34', padding: '1rem',
color: 'white' }}>
    <h1>Admin Dashboard</h1>
  </header>
);

export default Header;
```

Step 2: Define the Sidebar Component

```
// File: src/components/Sidebar.js
import React from 'react';
import CustomButton from './CustomButton';

const Sidebar = () => (
```

```
    <aside style={{ width: '200px', padding: '1rem',
background: '#f4f4f4' }}>
      <nav>
        <ul style={{ listStyle: 'none', padding: 0 }}>
          <li>
            <CustomButton label="Dashboard" onClick={() =>
console.log('Dashboard clicked')} />
          </li>
          <li style={{ marginTop: '1rem' }}>
            <CustomButton label="Settings" onClick={() =>
console.log('Settings clicked')} />
          </li>
        </ul>
      </nav>
    </aside>
);

export default Sidebar;
```

Step 3: Define the Content Component

```
// File: src/components/Content.js
import React from 'react';

const Content = () => (
  <main style={{ flex: 1, padding: '1rem' }}>
    <h2>Welcome to your dashboard!</h2>
    <p>This is where your content will be displayed.</p>
  </main>
);

export default Content;
```

Step 4: Compose the Dashboard Layout

```
// File: src/components/Dashboard.js
import React from 'react';
import Header from './Header';
import Sidebar from './Sidebar';
import Content from './Content';

const Dashboard = () => {
  return (
    <div style={{ display: 'flex', flexDirection: 'column',
minHeight: '100vh' }}>
      <Header />
      <div style={{ display: 'flex', flex: 1 }}>
        <Sidebar />
        <Content />
```

```
      </div>
    </div>
  );
};

export default Dashboard;
```

Explanation:

- **Modularity:**
  Each section of the dashboard is its own component. This makes it easier to modify the header, sidebar, or content without affecting the others.
- **Reuse:**
  The `CustomButton` we created earlier is used within the sidebar for navigation.
- **Layout:**
  The dashboard layout uses CSS flexbox to create a responsive design.

Best Practices for Component Composition

1. **Keep Components Focused:**
   Each component should have a single responsibility. If a component starts growing too large, consider breaking it into smaller parts.
2. **Use Children for Flexibility:**
   Leverage the `children` prop to allow components to render nested elements. For example, a `Card` component can render dynamic content passed as children.

```
// File: src/components/Card.js
import React from 'react';

const Card = ({ children, style }) => (
  <div style={{ border: '1px solid #ddd', padding: '1rem',
borderRadius: '4px', ...style }}>
    {children}
  </div>
);

export default Card;
```

3. **Prop Drilling vs. Context:**
   When you need to pass data through multiple levels of components, consider using React Context to avoid "prop drilling."
4. **Document Component APIs:**
   Clearly document the props and behaviors of your reusable components. This makes it easier for team members (or future you) to understand and reuse them.

Personal Insight:
I learned early on that investing time in designing reusable components not only speeds up development but also leads to a more predictable and maintainable codebase. Instead of rewriting similar code, you can build a library of components that serve as the building blocks for your application.

3.4: Styling Approaches: CSS, CSS-in-JS, and Material-UI

Styling in React is a broad subject with several powerful approaches to choose from. In this guide, we'll explore three popular methods: traditional CSS, CSS-in-JS (using a library like styled-components), and Material-UI. We'll discuss each method's benefits, trade-offs, and provide step-by-step, working code examples to help you decide which fits your project best.

Traditional CSS

Traditional CSS involves writing style rules in separate .css files and applying them via class names or IDs. This approach is familiar to many developers and works well for smaller projects or when you want to keep HTML and CSS clearly separated.

Step-by-Step Example

1. **Create a CSS File**

Create a file called `App.css` in your `src/` directory:

```css
/* File: src/App.css */
.container {
  padding: 2rem;
  text-align: center;
  background-color: #f9f9f9;
}

.title {
  color: #333;
  font-size: 2rem;
  margin-bottom: 1rem;
}

.button {
  background-color: #007bff;
  color: white;
  border: none;
  padding: 0.5rem 1rem;
  border-radius: 4px;
  cursor: pointer;
}

.button:hover {
  background-color: #0056b3;
}
```

2. **Apply the Styles in a React Component**

Update your `App.js` to use these CSS classes:

```js
// File: src/App.js
import React from 'react';
import './App.css';

const App = () => {
  return (
    <div className="container">
      <h1 className="title">Traditional CSS Styling</h1>
      <button className="button" onClick={() =>
alert('Button clicked!')}>
        Click Me
      </button>
    </div>
  );
};

export default App;
```

Pros:

- Familiar and straightforward.
- Separation of concerns: HTML and CSS are kept in distinct files.
- Wide browser support without additional dependencies.

Cons:

- Global scope can lead to naming conflicts.
- Styles are not scoped to components by default, making large projects harder to manage.

Personal Insight:
I appreciate the simplicity of traditional CSS when working on small projects or prototypes. However, as applications scale, managing a global CSS namespace can become challenging.

CSS-in-JS with styled-components

CSS-in-JS libraries like styled-components allow you to write your styles directly in your JavaScript files. This approach scopes styles to components automatically and makes it easy to manage dynamic styling based on props or state.

Step-by-Step Example

1. **Install styled-components**

   Run the following command in your project directory:

```
npm install styled-components
```

2. **Create a Styled Component**

   Create a new file called StyledApp.js:

```
// File: src/StyledApp.js
import React from 'react';
import styled from 'styled-components';
```

```
// Define styled components
const Container = styled.div`
  padding: 2rem;
  text-align: center;
  background-color: #f9f9f9;
`;

const Title = styled.h1`
  color: #333;
  font-size: 2rem;
  margin-bottom: 1rem;
`;

const Button = styled.button`
  background-color: #007bff;
  color: white;
  border: none;
  padding: 0.5rem 1rem;
  border-radius: 4px;
  cursor: pointer;
  &:hover {
    background-color: #0056b3;
  }
`;

const StyledApp = () => {
  return (
    <Container>
      <Title>CSS-in-JS with styled-components</Title>
      <Button onClick={() => alert('Styled Button
clicked!')}>Click Me</Button>
    </Container>
  );
};

export default StyledApp;
```

3. **Use the Styled Component in Your App**

   Update your entry point to render StyledApp instead of the
   traditional CSS version if desired.

Pros:

- Automatically scopes styles to components.
- Styles can be dynamic, reacting to props and state changes.
- Reduces the risk of naming conflicts.

Cons:

- Introduces an additional dependency.
- Can be less familiar if coming from a traditional CSS background.

Personal Insight:
I love how CSS-in-JS keeps everything together in one file. It makes refactoring much easier since the component logic and its styles live side by side. This approach really shines in complex applications where style encapsulation is key.

Material-UI

Material-UI is a comprehensive React UI framework that implements Google's Material Design. It provides a wide range of pre-built components that are highly customizable and consistent in design.

Step-by-Step Example

1. **Install Material-UI**

   Run the following command:

```
npm install @mui/material @emotion/react @emotion/styled
```

2. **Create a Component Using Material-UI**

   Create a new file called `MuiApp.js`:

```
// File: src/MuiApp.js
import React from 'react';
import { Button, Container, Typography, Card, CardContent }
from '@mui/material';

const MuiApp = () => {
  return (
    <Container style={{ padding: '2rem', textAlign:
'center' }}>
      <Card style={{ marginBottom: '1rem' }}>
        <CardContent>
          <Typography variant="h4" gutterBottom>
```

```
            Material-UI Styling
          </Typography>
          <Typography variant="body1">
            This component uses Material-UI components and
theming.
          </Typography>
        </CardContent>
      </Card>
      <Button variant="contained" color="primary"
onClick={() => alert('Material-UI Button clicked!')}>
        Click Me
      </Button>
    </Container>
  );
};

export default MuiApp;
```

3. **Integrate the Material-UI Component**

   Modify your main entry point to render `MuiApp` if you want to test Material-UI.

Pros:

- Provides a rich set of pre-styled components.
- Ensures consistency with Material Design guidelines.
- Highly customizable through theming and style overrides.

Cons:

- Can be overkill for simple projects.
- The learning curve might be steeper if you're not familiar with Material Design concepts.

Personal Insight:
Material-UI has been a lifesaver in projects where I needed a polished, professional look without spending too much time on custom design. Its extensive component library accelerates development and ensures a uniform design language across your application.

Each styling approach comes with its own set of advantages and trade-offs:

- **Traditional CSS** is great for simplicity and familiarity but may lead to conflicts in large projects.
- **CSS-in-JS (styled-components)** offers encapsulation and dynamic styling with a modern, integrated approach.
- **Material-UI** provides a robust, pre-designed component library that can significantly speed up development for professional applications.

The right choice depends on your project's needs, team preferences, and the complexity of your UI. Experiment with these methods, and consider mixing approaches if necessary—for instance, using Material-UI for complex components while keeping simpler parts styled with traditional CSS or CSS-in-JS.

Chapter 4: Creating Your First Admin Dashboard

In this chapter, we'll walk through the process of creating your first admin dashboard using React Admin. We'll explore the layout and core components, configure resource definitions, build complete CRUD views, and set up routing and navigation. By the end of this chapter, you'll have a functional admin dashboard that you can customize further for your needs.

4.1: Exploring the React Admin Layout and Core Components

React Admin is designed to simplify the creation of robust admin interfaces by abstracting many of the common tasks involved in data management and layout. In this section, we'll dive into the core components that power React Admin and examine how they work together to create a cohesive dashboard experience. We'll also walk through a practical, step-by-step example to solidify these concepts.

The Core of React Admin

At the heart of every React Admin application is the `<Admin>` component. Think of it as the central hub that coordinates your app's layout, routing, theming, and data integration. Here's a breakdown of the key components:

- **`<Admin>` Component:**
  This is the root component that sets up the admin interface. It takes in a data provider, which connects your app to your backend API, and manages global settings like the theme and authentication.
- **`<Resource>` Component:**
  This component represents a single data model (e.g., users, posts, products). For each resource, you can specify various views such as List, Create, Edit, and Show. React Admin automatically creates

routes and handles data operations based on the configuration provided.

- **CRUD Views (List, Create, Edit, Show):**
  React Admin provides pre-built components to handle the standard CRUD operations. These include:
    - `<List>`: Renders a list of records.
    - `<Create>`: Provides a form for adding new records.
    - `<Edit>`: Renders a form pre-populated with an existing record for updating.
    - `<Show>`: Displays the details of a single record.
- **Layout and Theming:**
  Out-of-the-box, React Admin uses Material-UI to provide a consistent and modern look. This means you get a responsive and accessible UI without having to write all the CSS from scratch.

Personal Insight:
When I first explored React Admin, I was struck by how much of the heavy lifting was done for me. The `<Admin>` component encapsulated so many best practices, from routing to theming, that I could focus more on building custom features rather than reinventing the wheel.

Step-by-Step: Building a Basic Admin Layout

Let's build a simple admin dashboard that lists posts from a demo API. This example will highlight the core components in action.

Step 1: Set Up the Data Provider

React Admin requires a data provider to fetch and manage data. In this example, we'll use `ra-data-json-server` to connect to the JSONPlaceholder API.

```
npm install react-admin ra-data-json-server
```

Step 2: Configure the `<Admin>` Component

Create an `App.js` file (or modify your existing one) to include the `<Admin>` component and configure it with the data provider.

```
// File: src/App.js
import React from 'react';
import { Admin, Resource } from 'react-admin';
import jsonServerProvider from 'ra-data-json-server';
import PostList from './posts/PostList'; // We will create
this component next

// Configure the data provider with the JSONPlaceholder API
const dataProvider =
jsonServerProvider('https://jsonplaceholder.typicode.com');

const App = () => (
  <Admin dataProvider={dataProvider}>
    {/* Define a resource for "posts" with a list view */}
    <Resource name="posts" list={PostList} />
  </Admin>
);

export default App;
```

Explanation:

- The `<Admin>` component wraps your entire admin interface.
- The `dataProvider` connects your app to the JSONPlaceholder API.
- The `<Resource>` component registers a "posts" resource and assigns it the `PostList` view for listing data.

Step 3: Create a List View for Posts

Now, create a simple list view to display posts. This view will use React Admin's `<List>` and `<Datagrid>` components.

```
// File: src/posts/PostList.js
import React from 'react';
import { List, Datagrid, TextField } from 'react-admin';

const PostList = () => (
  <List>
    <Datagrid rowClick="edit">
      <TextField source="id" label="ID" />
      <TextField source="title" label="Title" />
      <TextField source="body" label="Content" />
    </Datagrid>
  </List>
);
```

```
export default PostList;
```

Explanation:

- **<List>:** Sets up the list view including pagination and filtering (if needed).
- **<Datagrid>:** Displays the data in a tabular format. The `rowClick="edit"` property lets users click a row to navigate to an edit view (to be implemented later).
- **<TextField>:** Renders individual fields from the fetched posts.

Personal Insight:
This structure impressed me with its simplicity. Rather than manually handling data fetching and table creation, React Admin's pre-built components streamlined the process, allowing me to see results almost immediately.

Understanding the Layout and Theming

React Admin's layout is highly customizable. By default, it uses Material-UI's design principles, meaning your admin interface will be responsive and visually appealing with minimal effort. If needed, you can override the default theme or create custom layouts by extending the components provided by React Admin.

Customizing the Layout (Optional)

For instance, if you want to add a custom header or menu, you can do so by creating your own components and passing them as props to the <Admin> component. This flexibility is part of what makes React Admin so powerful.

```
// File: src/components/CustomHeader.js
import React from 'react';

const CustomHeader = () => (
  <div style={{ background: '#333', color: '#fff', padding:
'1rem', textAlign: 'center' }}>
    <h1>My Custom Admin Dashboard</h1>
  </div>
```

```
);

export default CustomHeader;
```

Then, integrate it in your `App.js` (if needed, by creating a custom layout). React Admin supports extensive customization, and as you grow more comfortable, you can tailor the experience to your exact needs.

Exploring the React Admin layout and core components is the first step toward building powerful admin interfaces. By leveraging the `<Admin>` and `<Resource>` components, along with pre-built CRUD views, you can rapidly assemble a functional dashboard. The combination of a well-thought-out data provider and a customizable layout means you can focus on delivering a great user experience rather than dealing with boilerplate code.

4.2: Configuring the Component and Resource Definitions

Configuring your admin interface starts with defining how your data is structured and how different parts of your application interact with that data. In React Admin, this process is primarily handled by the `<Resource>` component, which connects your UI with a backend data source through a data provider. In this guide, we'll explore how to configure component and resource definitions step by step, and explain the reasoning behind each decision.

Understanding Resources in React Admin

A **resource** represents a type of data your admin dashboard will manage (for example, posts, users, or products). Each resource typically includes a set of views such as a list, create, edit, and show view. When you define a resource, React Admin automatically creates routes and integrates CRUD functionalities based on the configuration you provide.

Key Points:

- **Modularity:** Each resource is isolated, which makes it easy to manage and scale as your application grows.
- **Automatic Routing:** By defining a resource, React Admin sets up the necessary routing to handle navigation between views.
- **Component Mapping:** You map specific components (like List, Create, Edit, and Show) to a resource to control how data is presented and managed.

Personal Insight:
When I first started using React Admin, the concept of resources simplified the way I thought about data. Instead of manually setting up routes and forms for every data type, I could define a resource and let the framework handle much of the heavy lifting. This approach not only streamlined my workflow but also kept my codebase organized.

Step-by-Step Guide to Configuring a Resource

Let's walk through configuring a resource for managing "posts" from a demo API.

Step 1: Set Up the Data Provider

Before defining your resource, you need a data provider that acts as a bridge between your admin dashboard and your backend API. In this example, we use `ra-data-json-server` to connect to the JSONPlaceholder API.

```
npm install ra-data-json-server
```

Then, configure your data provider in your main application file:

```js
// File: src/App.js
import React from 'react';
import { Admin, Resource } from 'react-admin';
import jsonServerProvider from 'ra-data-json-server';

// Set up the data provider with a demo API endpoint
const dataProvider =
jsonServerProvider('https://jsonplaceholder.typicode.com');

const App = () => (
```

```
  <Admin dataProvider={dataProvider}>
    {/* Resource definitions will be added here */}
  </Admin>
);

export default App;
```

Step 2: Create Resource-Specific Components

For our "posts" resource, we need to define the components for various
views. Let's start with a basic list view.

A. Creating the List View
```
// File: src/posts/PostList.js
import React from 'react';
import { List, Datagrid, TextField } from 'react-admin';

const PostList = () => (
  <List>
    <Datagrid rowClick="edit">
      <TextField source="id" label="ID" />
      <TextField source="title" label="Title" />
      <TextField source="body" label="Content" />
    </Datagrid>
  </List>
);

export default PostList;
```

Explanation:

- **<List>:** Sets up the container for the list view, including built-in
  pagination and filtering.
- **<Datagrid>:** Organizes the data into a table layout. The
  rowClick="edit" prop lets users click on any row to navigate to
  the edit view.
- **<TextField>:** Displays individual data fields.

B. (Optional) Create Other CRUD Views

While you might start with a list view, it's common to add Create, Edit,
and Show views to fully manage your resource.

Create View Example:

```
// File: src/posts/PostCreate.js
import React from 'react';
import { Create, SimpleForm, TextInput } from 'react-admin';

const PostCreate = () => (
  <Create>
    <SimpleForm>
      <TextInput source="title" label="Title" />
      <TextInput source="body" label="Content" multiline />
    </SimpleForm>
  </Create>
);

export default PostCreate;
```

Edit View Example:

```
// File: src/posts/PostEdit.js
import React from 'react';
import { Edit, SimpleForm, TextInput } from 'react-admin';

const PostEdit = () => (
  <Edit>
    <SimpleForm>
      <TextInput disabled source="id" label="ID" />
      <TextInput source="title" label="Title" />
      <TextInput source="body" label="Content" multiline />
    </SimpleForm>
  </Edit>
);

export default PostEdit;
```

Show View Example:

```
// File: src/posts/PostShow.js
import React from 'react';
import { Show, SimpleShowLayout, TextField } from 'react-admin';

const PostShow = () => (
  <Show>
    <SimpleShowLayout>
      <TextField source="id" label="ID" />
      <TextField source="title" label="Title" />
      <TextField source="body" label="Content" />
    </SimpleShowLayout>
  </Show>
```

```
);

export default PostShow;
```

Step 3: Register the Resource

Now that you have your components ready, register the "posts" resource in your main `App.js` file. This step ties your components to the resource so that React Admin can automatically generate routes and integrate the data provider.

```javascript
// File: src/App.js
import React from 'react';
import { Admin, Resource } from 'react-admin';
import jsonServerProvider from 'ra-data-json-server';
import PostList from './posts/PostList';
import PostCreate from './posts/PostCreate';
import PostEdit from './posts/PostEdit';
import PostShow from './posts/PostShow';

// Configure the data provider with the demo API endpoint
const dataProvider =
jsonServerProvider('https://jsonplaceholder.typicode.com');

const App = () => (
  <Admin dataProvider={dataProvider}>
    <Resource
      name="posts"
      list={PostList}
      create={PostCreate}
      edit={PostEdit}
      show={PostShow}
    />
  </Admin>
);

export default App;
```

Explanation:

- The `<Resource>` component is configured with the name "posts", which tells React Admin which endpoints to use.
- The views (`list`, `create`, `edit`, `show`) are mapped to their respective components, enabling full CRUD operations for this resource.

Best Practices and Additional Tips

- **Separation of Concerns:**
  Keep your resource-specific components (like PostList, PostEdit) in their own folders (e.g., `src/posts/`). This organization improves readability and maintainability.
- **Consistent Naming:**
  Use clear and consistent naming conventions for your resources and components. This helps both you and your team understand the structure at a glance.
- **Incremental Enhancement:**
  Start by defining only the necessary views. As your application requirements grow, you can incrementally add and refine components without needing to overhaul your entire resource configuration.

Personal Insight:
When working on my first React Admin project, organizing resource definitions was a turning point. Instead of scattering related functionalities, grouping them by resource made the codebase much more manageable. This organization also simplified debugging and future enhancements, which is crucial for long-term project success.

4.3: Building CRUD Views: List, Create, Edit, and Show

CRUD—Create, Read, Update, and Delete—is the backbone of any data-driven application. In React Admin, building these views is streamlined with pre-built components that allow you to focus on customizing the UI rather than reinventing standard functionalities. In this section, we'll walk through each of these views step by step, using a "posts" resource as an example. Along the way, I'll share insights on how these components work together to form a comprehensive admin interface.

The List View

The List view displays a collection of records in a user-friendly format, usually in a table. React Admin provides the `<List>` and `<Datagrid>` components to handle this effortlessly.

Step-by-Step Implementation

1. Create the List Component:

```
// File: src/posts/PostList.js
import React from 'react';
import { List, Datagrid, TextField } from 'react-admin';

const PostList = () => (
  <List>
    <Datagrid rowClick="edit">
      <TextField source="id" label="ID" />
      <TextField source="title" label="Title" />
      <TextField source="body" label="Content" />
    </Datagrid>
  </List>
);

export default PostList;
```

Explanation:

- o **`<List>`:** Wraps the view and provides built-in functionalities like pagination and filters.
- o **`<Datagrid>`:** Displays records in a table format. The `rowClick="edit"` prop makes rows clickable to navigate to the Edit view.
- o **`<TextField>`:** Renders specific fields from each record.

Personal Insight:
I appreciate how the List view abstracts away the complexities of table creation. With minimal code, you can have a fully functional list that supports sorting and filtering.

The Create View

The Create view allows users to add new records. React Admin's `<Create>` component, combined with `<SimpleForm>`, simplifies building forms for data entry.

Step-by-Step Implementation

1. Create the Create Component:

```
// File: src/posts/PostCreate.js
import React from 'react';
import { Create, SimpleForm, TextInput } from 'react-admin';

const PostCreate = () => (
  <Create>
    <SimpleForm>
      <TextInput source="title" label="Title" />
      <TextInput source="body" label="Content" multiline />
    </SimpleForm>
  </Create>
);

export default PostCreate;
```

Explanation:

- **`<Create>`:** Sets up the creation mode and handles submission logic.
- **`<SimpleForm>`:** Provides a simple form layout.
- **`<TextInput>`:** Renders input fields for different attributes. The `multiline` prop allows for longer text entries.

Personal Insight:
Using `<Create>` and `<SimpleForm>` has dramatically reduced the time I spent on building forms from scratch. It handles validation and submission for you, so you can focus on customizing the fields.

The Edit View

The Edit view is similar to the Create view but is designed to update existing records. It pre-fills the form with current data and allows modifications.

Step-by-Step Implementation

1. **Create the Edit Component:**

```
// File: src/posts/PostEdit.js
import React from 'react';
import { Edit, SimpleForm, TextInput } from 'react-admin';

const PostEdit = () => (
  <Edit>
    <SimpleForm>
      <TextInput disabled source="id" label="ID" />
      <TextInput source="title" label="Title" />
      <TextInput source="body" label="Content" multiline />
    </SimpleForm>
  </Edit>
);

export default PostEdit;
```

Explanation:

- **<Edit>:** Similar to <Create>, but for updating records. It automatically loads the existing data.
- **<SimpleForm>:** Provides a familiar form layout.
- **Disabled Input:** The ID field is disabled to prevent editing the primary key, which is typically not changeable.

Personal Insight:
The consistency between Create and Edit views in React Admin allows for a seamless development experience. Once you understand one, adapting to the other is almost second nature.

The Show View

The Show view presents a detailed read-only view of a single record. This is useful for viewing all data attributes without the risk of accidental edits.

Step-by-Step Implementation

1. Create the Show Component:

```
// File: src/posts/PostShow.js
import React from 'react';
import { Show, SimpleShowLayout, TextField } from 'react-admin';

const PostShow = () => (
  <Show>
    <SimpleShowLayout>
      <TextField source="id" label="ID" />
      <TextField source="title" label="Title" />
      <TextField source="body" label="Content" />
    </SimpleShowLayout>
  </Show>
);

export default PostShow;
```

Explanation:

- **<Show>:** Initiates the read-only mode for displaying detailed record information.
- **<SimpleShowLayout>:** Arranges the fields in a clear, vertical layout.
- **<TextField>:** Renders each attribute for easy viewing.

Personal Insight:
The Show view is invaluable when you want to quickly inspect a record without the distractions of a form. Its layout is simple, yet effective for presenting data clearly.

Integrating CRUD Views into Your Admin Dashboard

With your CRUD views ready, the final step is to register them with the <Resource> component in your main application file.

```
// File: src/App.js
```

```
import React from 'react';
import { Admin, Resource } from 'react-admin';
import jsonServerProvider from 'ra-data-json-server';
import PostList from './posts/PostList';
import PostCreate from './posts/PostCreate';
import PostEdit from './posts/PostEdit';
import PostShow from './posts/PostShow';

const dataProvider =
jsonServerProvider('https://jsonplaceholder.typicode.com');

const App = () => (
  <Admin dataProvider={dataProvider}>
    <Resource
      name="posts"
      list={PostList}
      create={PostCreate}
      edit={PostEdit}
      show={PostShow}
    />
  </Admin>
);

export default App;
```

Explanation:

- **Resource Registration:**
  The `<Resource>` component maps your CRUD views to the
  "posts" resource. React Admin automatically generates the
  necessary routes, so users can navigate between listing, creating,
  editing, and showing posts.

Personal Insight:
Seeing the entire CRUD interface come together was immensely
satisfying. This structure not only accelerates development but also
provides a solid, consistent framework that scales as your project grows.

Building CRUD views in React Admin is a systematic process that
leverages pre-built components to handle common data operations. By
breaking down the functionality into List, Create, Edit, and Show views,
you create a robust and user-friendly interface with minimal effort. Each
view is designed to handle specific aspects of data management, and when
combined, they form a comprehensive admin dashboard.

I encourage you to experiment with these examples and customize them to fit your project's needs. As you grow more comfortable with these components, you'll find that React Admin offers a powerful, efficient way to manage and present data.

Part II: Enhancing the Dashboard with Intermediate Techniques

Chapter 5: Implementing Responsive Design

Responsive design is essential for building admin dashboards that work seamlessly across devices—whether on large desktop screens or mobile devices. In this chapter, we'll explore the principles behind responsive web design, learn how to integrate Material-UI for adaptive layouts, use media queries and theming for a consistent user experience, and cover best practices for mobile-first development.

Personal Insight:
Early in my career, I underestimated the importance of responsiveness. When users began accessing our dashboards on mobile devices, it became clear that a well-thought-out responsive design was not a luxury but a necessity. Today, I find that designing with a mobile-first mindset results in cleaner, more intuitive interfaces.

5.1: Principles of Responsive Web Design

Responsive web design is the art and science of crafting web experiences that adapt seamlessly to a range of devices and screen sizes. Whether your users are on a smartphone, tablet, or desktop, the goal is to ensure that your interface remains clear, usable, and engaging. In this guide, we'll break down the core principles of responsive design, explain how they work together, and provide practical, step-by-step examples to illustrate each concept.

Core Principles of Responsive Web Design

1. Fluid Grids

What It Means:
Fluid grids allow your layout to adjust dynamically to the width of the

viewport by using relative units (like percentages or ems) instead of fixed pixel values.

Why It's Important:
A fluid grid ensures that your content reflows naturally on different screen sizes. This means that instead of having a fixed width, your layout scales up or down, maintaining balance and readability.

Example:

```css
/* File: src/App.css */

/* Base container style using a fluid grid */
.container {
  width: 100%;              /* Full width of the viewport */
  max-width: 1200px;        /* Optional maximum width */
  margin: 0 auto;           /* Center the container */
  padding: 1rem;
}

/* Grid system for columns */
.row {
  display: flex;
  flex-wrap: wrap;
  margin: 0 -0.5rem;        /* Negative margin to offset
padding on columns */
}

.column {
  flex: 1 1 100%;           /* Default to full width on small
screens */
  padding: 0 0.5rem;
}

/* Adjust columns for larger screens */
@media (min-width: 768px) {
  .column {
    flex: 1 1 50%;          /* Two columns side by side */
  }
}

@media (min-width: 1024px) {
  .column {
    flex: 1 1 33.33%;       /* Three columns on larger
screens */
  }
}
```

Personal Insight:
When I started designing interfaces, switching to fluid grids was a revelation. Suddenly, layouts that once looked awkward on mobile devices transformed into flexible, user-friendly designs. This adaptability is what makes a design truly modern.

2. Flexible Images and Media

What It Means:
Images and other media should resize within their containing elements to prevent overflow and maintain layout integrity.

Why It's Important:
Without flexibility, images might stretch beyond their containers on smaller devices, leading to horizontal scrolling or distorted visuals.

Example:

```
/* File: src/App.css */

/* Ensure images are responsive */
img {
  max-width: 100%;    /* Scale down if necessary */
  height: auto;       /* Maintain aspect ratio */
}
```

Personal Insight:
I've encountered many projects where images broke the layout on mobile. Implementing responsive image styles not only improves aesthetics but also enhances user experience, especially on slower networks.

3. Media Queries

What It Means:
Media queries let you apply different styles based on the characteristics of the device, such as its width, height, or orientation.

Why It's Important:
They allow you to fine-tune the design for different devices, ensuring that text, images, and layout elements look great no matter the screen size.

Example:

```
/* File: src/App.css */

/* Base styles for mobile-first design */
body {
  font-size: 14px;
  padding: 1rem;
}

/* Adjust styles for tablets and larger devices */
@media (min-width: 600px) {
  body {
    font-size: 16px;
    padding: 2rem;
  }
}

/* Further adjustments for desktops */
@media (min-width: 960px) {
  body {
    font-size: 18px;
    padding: 3rem;
  }
}
```

Personal Insight:
Media queries are like the tuning knobs of web design. They allow you to polish the experience for different devices, and over time, you develop an intuitive sense of the breakpoints that work best for your design.

---

4. Progressive Enhancement

What It Means:
Progressive enhancement starts with a baseline experience that works on all devices, then adds layers of enhancements for devices that can support them.

Why It's Important:
This approach ensures that your website is accessible to everyone, regardless of device capability or network speed, while still offering a rich experience for those on more advanced systems.

Example:

```html
<!-- File: public/index.html -->
<!DOCTYPE html>
<html lang="en">
<head>
  <meta charset="UTF-8">
  <meta name="viewport" content="width=device-width,
initial-scale=1.0">
  <title>Progressive Enhancement Example</title>
  <link rel="stylesheet" href="App.css">
</head>
<body>
  <div class="container">
    <h1>Welcome to My Responsive Site</h1>
    <p>This is the baseline experience available to all
users.</p>
  </div>
</body>
</html>
```

Then, add enhancements in your CSS with media queries as shown above.

Personal Insight:
Adopting a progressive enhancement mindset early in your design process means your application is built for the lowest common denominator first—ensuring accessibility and performance—and then you enhance it as much as possible. It's a philosophy that has served me well in creating robust, user-centric applications.

The principles of responsive web design—fluid grids, flexible images, media queries, and progressive enhancement—work together to create an adaptable, user-friendly interface that shines on any device. By understanding and implementing these principles, you can ensure that your admin dashboard and other web applications are accessible, aesthetically pleasing, and functional across a wide range of environments.

5.2: Integrating Material-UI for Adaptive Layouts

Material-UI (MUI) is a popular React UI framework that brings Google's Material Design to your projects. It provides a rich set of pre-built, customizable components and a robust grid system that makes it easier to build adaptive layouts. In this guide, we'll explore how to integrate Material-UI into your React application to create layouts that adapt seamlessly to different screen sizes. We'll walk through the process step by step, including installation, setting up a responsive grid layout, and using Material-UI's theming capabilities.

Why Material-UI?

Material-UI offers several advantages when building adaptive layouts:

- **Pre-built Components:** Quickly build interfaces with components like Grid, Container, Paper, and Typography.
- **Responsive Grid System:** Design layouts that adjust fluidly to various screen sizes.
- **Customizable Themes:** Easily tweak colors, spacing, and breakpoints to match your brand.
- **Consistency:** Material-UI components adhere to Material Design principles, ensuring a polished, uniform look.

Personal Insight:
I've found Material-UI to be a game-changer in creating responsive designs. Its grid system and pre-designed components allow me to focus on functionality and user experience rather than reinventing the wheel with custom CSS. The result is professional, cohesive interfaces that work well on both mobile and desktop.

Step 1: Install Material-UI

Before you can use Material-UI, install the necessary packages in your React project. Open your terminal in the project directory and run:

```
npm install @mui/material @emotion/react @emotion/styled
```

This command installs:

- **@mui/material:** The core Material-UI components.
- **@emotion/react & @emotion/styled:** Emotion is used for styling components and is the default styling engine for Material-UI v5.

Step 2: Create a Responsive Layout Using Material-UI Components

Material-UI's `Grid` and `Container` components simplify creating responsive layouts. Let's build a basic dashboard layout that adapts to different screen sizes.

Example: Responsive Dashboard Layout

Create a new file named `ResponsiveDashboard.js` in your `src/components` folder:

```javascript
// File: src/components/ResponsiveDashboard.js
import React from 'react';
import { Container, Grid, Paper, Typography } from
'@mui/material';

const ResponsiveDashboard = () => {
  return (
    <Container maxWidth="lg" style={{ marginTop: '2rem' }}>
      <Grid container spacing={3}>
        {/* Header */}
        <Grid item xs={12}>
          <Paper style={{ padding: '1rem' }}>
            <Typography variant="h4" align="center">
              Admin Dashboard
            </Typography>
          </Paper>
        </Grid>

        {/* Sidebar */}
```

```
            <Grid item xs={12} md={3}>
              <Paper style={{ padding: '1rem' }}>
                <Typography
variant="h6">Navigation</Typography>
                {/* Navigation items can be added here */}
              </Paper>
            </Grid>

            {/* Main Content */}
            <Grid item xs={12} md={9}>
              <Paper style={{ padding: '1rem' }}>
                <Typography variant="h6">Dashboard
Content</Typography>
                {/* Main content goes here */}
              </Paper>
            </Grid>
          </Grid>
        </Container>
    );
};

export default ResponsiveDashboard;
```

Explanation:

- **Container:**
  The `<Container>` component centers your content and sets a maximum width (in this case, `"lg"` for large screens). It also adds horizontal padding automatically.
- **Grid System:**
  - `<Grid container spacing={3}>` creates a grid container with a spacing of 3 (theme spacing units) between items.
  - Grid items use the `xs` and `md` props to define how many columns they take up. For example, the sidebar is full-width on extra-small devices (`xs={12}`) and 3 columns (out of 12) on medium and larger devices (`md={3}`).
- **Paper & Typography:**
  The `<Paper>` component provides a subtle elevation (shadow) and a clean background for content blocks, while `<Typography>` handles text styling in a consistent manner.

Personal Insight:
I enjoy using Material-UI's grid system because it simplifies responsive design. Instead of writing complex CSS media queries, you can let the

Grid component handle most of the heavy lifting. This approach leads to faster prototyping and cleaner code.

Step 3: Customizing with Material-UI Themes

Material-UI allows you to define a custom theme that adjusts colors, spacing, and breakpoints across your application. This ensures a consistent look and feel.

Creating a Custom Theme

Create a file named theme.js in your src directory:

```
// File: src/theme.js
import { createTheme } from '@mui/material/styles';

const theme = createTheme({
  breakpoints: {
    values: {
      xs: 0,
      sm: 600,
      md: 960,
      lg: 1280,
      xl: 1920,
    },
  },
  palette: {
    primary: {
      main: '#1976d2', // Customize primary color
    },
    secondary: {
      main: '#dc004e', // Customize secondary color
    },
  },
  typography: {
    fontFamily: '"Roboto", "Helvetica", "Arial", sans-
serif',
  },
});

export default theme;
```

Applying the Custom Theme

Wrap your application in a `ThemeProvider` in your entry point, typically `src/index.js`:

```
// File: src/index.js
import React from 'react';
import ReactDOM from 'react-dom';
import { ThemeProvider } from '@mui/material/styles';
import App from './App';
import theme from './theme';

ReactDOM.render(
  <React.StrictMode>
    <ThemeProvider theme={theme}>
      <App />
    </ThemeProvider>
  </React.StrictMode>,
  document.getElementById('root')
);
```

Explanation:

- **ThemeProvider:**
  The `ThemeProvider` component makes the theme available to all Material-UI components within your application.
- **Custom Theme:**
  By customizing the theme, you can ensure consistent styling across your dashboard—such as setting your brand colors and adjusting breakpoints for responsiveness.

Personal Insight:
Defining a custom theme early in your project helped me maintain a consistent design language across all components. It was especially useful when working with multiple team members, ensuring everyone was on the same page regarding design guidelines.

5.3: Using Media Queries and Theming for Consistent UX

A consistent user experience (UX) is the cornerstone of any successful web application. Whether users are accessing your admin dashboard on a small smartphone or a large desktop monitor, your design should feel cohesive and intuitive. In this section, we'll dive into two powerful tools to help achieve that goal: media queries and theming.

We'll cover what media queries are, how to use them to adjust your layout and styles for various screen sizes, and then discuss how theming—using tools like Material-UI or even CSS custom properties—can keep your design consistent throughout your application. Throughout, I'll share step-by-step examples and personal insights to illustrate these key concepts.

What Are Media Queries?

Media queries allow you to apply CSS styles selectively based on characteristics of the device or display, such as screen width, resolution, or orientation. They are a critical component of responsive design.

How Media Queries Work

Media queries enable you to define breakpoints in your CSS. For example, you might have different font sizes, margins, or layouts for mobile devices (small screens) versus desktops (large screens).

Step-by-Step Example: Basic Media Queries

Imagine you have a simple container that should have different padding on mobile versus desktop devices. Here's how you might write that:

```css
/* File: src/App.css */

/* Base styles for mobile-first design */
.container {
  padding: 1rem;
  background-color: #f9f9f9;
  text-align: center;
}

/* Enhance layout for tablets and larger devices */
@media (min-width: 600px) {
  .container {
    padding: 2rem;
  }
}
```

```
/* Further adjustments for desktops */
@media (min-width: 960px) {
  .container {
    padding: 3rem;
  }
}
```

Explanation:

- **Mobile-First Approach:** We start with the smallest layout. The base styles apply to all devices.
- **Breakpoints:**
  - At 600px (typical for tablets), we increase the padding.
  - At 960px (desktop screens), we further increase the padding.

Personal Insight:
When I first started using media queries, I appreciated the control they gave me over my layout. They allowed me to incrementally enhance the user interface without rewriting the entire design for each device type.

Theming for Consistent UX

Theming goes hand in hand with responsive design by ensuring that your visual design—colors, typography, spacing, and more—remains consistent across your application. Using a centralized theme not only makes it easier to maintain your styles but also speeds up development.

Theming with Material-UI

Material-UI (MUI) makes theming simple by providing a `ThemeProvider` and a flexible `createTheme` function. With Material-UI, you can define breakpoints, colors, typography, and other design tokens in a single place.

Step-by-Step Example: Creating and Applying a Custom Theme

1. **Create a Custom Theme**

Create a file called `theme.js`:

```
// File: src/theme.js
import { createTheme } from '@mui/material/styles';

const theme = createTheme({
  breakpoints: {
    values: {
      xs: 0,
      sm: 600,
      md: 960,
      lg: 1280,
      xl: 1920,
    },
  },
  palette: {
    primary: {
      main: '#1976d2', // Your brand primary color
    },
    secondary: {
      main: '#dc004e', // Your brand secondary color
    },
  },
  typography: {
    fontFamily: '"Roboto", "Helvetica", "Arial", sans-
serif',
  },
});

export default theme;
```

2. Apply the Theme to Your Application

Wrap your main app component with Material-UI's `ThemeProvider` in `index.js`:

```
// File: src/index.js
import React from 'react';
import ReactDOM from 'react-dom';
import { ThemeProvider } from '@mui/material/styles';
import App from './App';
import theme from './theme';

ReactDOM.render(
  <React.StrictMode>
    <ThemeProvider theme={theme}>
      <App />
    </ThemeProvider>
  </React.StrictMode>,
  document.getElementById('root')
);
```

Explanation:

- **Centralized Design:** All Material-UI components now use your custom theme, ensuring a consistent look and feel.
- **Breakpoints in Theme:** The breakpoints defined in your theme can be used within your components when using Material-UI's styling solutions.

Using CSS Custom Properties for Theming (Optional)

If you're not using Material-UI, CSS custom properties (variables) provide another powerful theming solution. Define your theme in a central CSS file and use the variables throughout your styles.

Step-by-Step Example: CSS Custom Properties

1. **Define Theme Variables**

Create a file called `variables.css`:

```css
/* File: src/variables.css */
:root {
  --primary-color: #1976d2;
  --secondary-color: #dc004e;
  --font-family: 'Roboto, Helvetica, Arial, sans-serif';
  --base-padding: 1rem;
  --tablet-padding: 2rem;
  --desktop-padding: 3rem;
}
```

2. **Use Variables in Your CSS**

Reference these variables in your styles:

```css
/* File: src/App.css */
@import './variables.css';

.container {
  padding: var(--base-padding);
  background-color: #f9f9f9;
  font-family: var(--font-family);
  text-align: center;
}

@media (min-width: 600px) {
```

```css
  .container {
    padding: var(--tablet-padding);
  }
}

@media (min-width: 960px) {
  .container {
    padding: var(--desktop-padding);
  }
}
```

Explanation:

- **Consistency:** Using CSS variables ensures that any changes to your theme (e.g., adjusting the primary color) are reflected everywhere they are used.
- **Ease of Maintenance:** You only need to update the value in one place, and the change cascades through your entire application.

Personal Insight:
I enjoy the flexibility of CSS custom properties for smaller projects or when I don't need the full power of a UI framework. They're incredibly lightweight and perfect for maintaining consistency with minimal overhead.

Using media queries and theming together creates a robust foundation for a consistent user experience across all devices. Media queries allow your layout and styles to adapt gracefully to different screen sizes, while theming—whether through Material-UI or CSS custom properties—ensures that your design language remains consistent throughout your application.

5.4: Best Practices for Mobile-First Development

Mobile-first development is an approach that starts with designing for the smallest screens and progressively enhances the experience as screen sizes increase. This philosophy ensures that your application is accessible, performant, and user-friendly on all devices—from smartphones to desktops. In this guide, we'll explore the best practices for mobile-first development, dive into practical code examples, and discuss strategies to create intuitive, touch-friendly interfaces.

What Does Mobile-First Mean?

Mobile-first design means starting with the essential features and a simplified layout for mobile devices, where screen real estate is limited. As the viewport grows, additional features and more complex layouts can be added. This ensures that your application performs well on slower networks and smaller screens, while still offering a rich experience on larger devices.

Key Principles:

- **Prioritize Essential Content:**
  Start by focusing on the most critical features and content. This ensures that even on a small screen, users get the information they need.
- **Optimize for Performance:**
  Mobile devices often have slower connections and less processing power. Prioritize loading speed, minimize heavy scripts, and optimize images.
- **Touch-Friendly Interactions:**
  Ensure that interactive elements (like buttons and links) are large enough to tap easily without accidental clicks.
- **Progressive Enhancement:**
  Build a strong foundation that works on all devices, then add enhancements for larger screens or more capable devices.

Personal Insight:
Early in my career, I focused on desktop designs without considering mobile users. Once I shifted to a mobile-first approach, I noticed significant improvements in performance and usability. It forces you to prioritize what truly matters and create lean, efficient designs.

Step-by-Step: Implementing Mobile-First Best Practices

1. Start with a Mobile-First CSS Approach

Begin by writing CSS for the smallest screens first. Use relative units and keep the design simple.

Example: Basic Mobile-First Layout

```css
/* File: src/App.css */

/* Base styles for mobile devices */
body {
  font-family: 'Arial', sans-serif;
  margin: 0;
  padding: 1rem;
  background-color: #f0f0f0;
}

.header, .content, .footer {
  padding: 1rem;
  background-color: #fff;
  margin-bottom: 1rem;
}

/* Mobile navigation menu */
.nav {
  display: flex;
  flex-direction: column;
  gap: 0.5rem;
}

.nav a {
  text-decoration: none;
  color: #1976d2;
  padding: 0.75rem;
  background-color: #e3f2fd;
  border-radius: 4px;
}

/* Enhance layout for tablets and up */
@media (min-width: 600px) {
  .container {
    max-width: 600px;
    margin: 0 auto;
  }
```

```
  /* Horizontal navigation for larger screens */
  .nav {
    flex-direction: row;
    justify-content: space-around;
  }
}

/* Further enhancements for desktops */
@media (min-width: 960px) {
  .container {
    max-width: 960px;
  }

  .header, .content, .footer {
    padding: 2rem;
  }
}
```

Explanation:

- **Mobile-First Base:** The base styles target small screens. The layout is simple and optimized for touch.
- **Media Queries:** Enhance the layout for larger devices by adjusting widths, padding, and navigation direction.
- **Relative Sizing:** Using rem and percentages ensures the layout adapts to different device settings.

2. Create Touch-Friendly Components

Ensure interactive elements are large enough and spaced appropriately for touch interactions.

Example: Responsive Button Component
```
// File: src/components/ResponsiveButton.js
import React from 'react';

const ResponsiveButton = ({ label, onClick }) => {
  return (
    <button
      onClick={onClick}
      style={{
        padding: '1rem 1.5rem',
        fontSize: '1rem',
        border: 'none',
        borderRadius: '5px',
        backgroundColor: '#1976d2',
        color: '#fff',
```

```
        cursor: 'pointer',
        width: '100%', // Full-width on mobile for easier
tapping
        maxWidth: '300px',
        margin: '0 auto',
        display: 'block'
      }}
    >
      {label}
    </button>
  );
};

export default ResponsiveButton;
```

Explanation:

- **Padding and Font Size:** Larger touch areas and legible text.
- **Full-Width on Mobile:** Improves accessibility by making buttons easier to tap on small screens.
- **Responsive Sizing:** The `maxWidth` ensures the button doesn't stretch too much on larger screens.

3. Optimize Performance for Mobile

Performance is crucial on mobile devices. Use techniques like image optimization, lazy loading, and minimizing JavaScript.

Example: Lazy Loading Images
```
// File: src/components/LazyImage.js
import React from 'react';

const LazyImage = ({ src, alt, ...props }) => {
  return (
    <img
      src={src}
      alt={alt}
      loading="lazy" // Native lazy loading
      style={{ maxWidth: '100%', height: 'auto', display:
'block', margin: '0 auto' }}
      {...props}
    />
  );
};

export default LazyImage;
```

Explanation:

- `loading="lazy"`: Instructs the browser to lazy-load the image, improving initial load times.
- **Responsive Styles:** Ensures the image scales properly on all devices.

4. Test on Real Devices and Emulators

Regularly test your design on various devices and screen sizes using browser developer tools or physical devices. Tools like Chrome's DevTools device toolbar can simulate different screen sizes, but nothing beats testing on an actual device.

Personal Insight:
I learned early on that designs can look great in a desktop browser but fall short on actual devices. Testing on real smartphones and tablets has saved me countless hours of troubleshooting and ensured that the final product is truly user-friendly.

Best Practices Summary

- **Design Mobile-First:** Start with a clean, simple base for small screens, then progressively enhance for larger screens.
- **Use Relative Units:** Embrace percentages, rems, and ems to ensure elements scale correctly.
- **Optimize Touch Interactions:** Make buttons and links large and accessible.
- **Enhance Performance:** Lazy-load images, minimize heavy scripts, and keep layouts lean.
- **Test Thoroughly:** Regularly use both emulators and real devices to ensure a seamless experience.

Adopting a mobile-first development approach is essential in today's multi-device world. By using media queries and theming together, you can craft designs that adapt gracefully to any screen size, ensuring a consistent and delightful user experience. The step-by-step examples provided here are meant to serve as a practical guide—experiment with them, tailor the breakpoints and styles to your project's needs, and enjoy building interfaces that perform beautifully on every device.

Chapter 6: Intermediate State Management Techniques

Managing state effectively is essential for building scalable and maintainable React applications. In this chapter, we dive into intermediate state management techniques beyond simple local state. We'll cover how to manage local state using Hooks, share state across components using the React Context API, implement more complex state logic with the `useReducer` Hook, and explore how React Admin offers built-in state patterns to simplify common tasks. Let's get started!

6.1: Managing Local State with Hooks

Functional components rely on Hooks to handle local state without the complexity of class-based components. The `useState` Hook is the most fundamental tool for managing state locally.

Key Concepts:

- **useState:** Allows you to declare a state variable and a function to update it.
- **Encapsulation:** Each component's state is isolated, making components self-contained and predictable.

Practical Example: A Counter Component

```
// File: src/components/Counter.js
import React, { useState } from 'react';

const Counter = () => {
  // Declare a state variable 'count' with an initial value
of 0
  const [count, setCount] = useState(0);

  return (
    <div style={{ textAlign: 'center', marginTop: '2rem'
}}>
      <h2>Current Count: {count}</h2>
```

```
        <button onClick={() => setCount(count + 1)} style={{
marginRight: '0.5rem' }}>
          Increase
        </button>
        <button onClick={() => setCount(count - 1)}>
          Decrease
        </button>
      </div>
    );
  };

export default Counter;
```

Explanation:

- The useState Hook initializes count to 0 and provides setCount to update the value.
- Each button click triggers an update, causing React to re-render the component with the new state.

Personal Insight:
Using useState was a turning point for me; it made handling dynamic values straightforward and helped me think in terms of data flows rather than component lifecycles.

6.2: Sharing State with React Context API

When you need to share state across multiple components without prop drilling, the React Context API is a powerful solution.

Key Concepts:

- **Context Provider:** Wraps your component tree and supplies a context value.
- **useContext Hook:** Allows components to consume the context value.

Practical Example: A Theme Context

1. Create the Context Provider

```
// File: src/contexts/ThemeContext.js
import React, { createContext, useState } from 'react';

export const ThemeContext = createContext();

export const ThemeProvider = ({ children }) => {
  const [theme, setTheme] = useState('light'); // 'light'
or 'dark'

  const toggleTheme = () => {
    setTheme((prevTheme) => (prevTheme === 'light' ? 'dark'
: 'light'));
  };

  return (
    <ThemeContext.Provider value={{ theme, toggleTheme }}>
      {children}
    </ThemeContext.Provider>
  );
};
```

2. Consume the Context in a Component

```
// File: src/components/ThemeToggler.js
import React, { useContext } from 'react';
import { ThemeContext } from '../contexts/ThemeContext';

const ThemeToggler = () => {
  const { theme, toggleTheme } = useContext(ThemeContext);

  return (
    <div style={{ textAlign: 'center', marginTop: '1rem'
}}>
      <p>Current Theme: {theme}</p>
      <button onClick={toggleTheme}>Toggle Theme</button>
    </div>
  );
};

export default ThemeToggler;
```

3. Wrap Your Application with the Provider

```
// File: src/index.js
import React from 'react';
import ReactDOM from 'react-dom';
import App from './App';
```

103

```
import { ThemeProvider } from './contexts/ThemeContext';

ReactDOM.render(
  <React.StrictMode>
    <ThemeProvider>
      <App />
    </ThemeProvider>
  </React.StrictMode>,
  document.getElementById('root')
);
```

Explanation:

- The `ThemeContext` is created and provided to the component tree.
- The `ThemeToggler` component consumes the context to display and change the theme.

Personal Insight:
The Context API has been a lifesaver in larger projects. It eliminates the need for deep prop drilling and centralizes state management for shared values like themes, user information, or language settings.

6.3: Advanced Patterns with useReducer

For more complex state logic, `useReducer` is a great alternative to `useState`. It's similar to Redux but built into React, providing a predictable state update mechanism based on dispatched actions.

Key Concepts:

- **Reducer Function:** Takes the current state and an action, then returns the new state.
- **Dispatch:** A function used to send actions to the reducer.

Practical Example: A Counter with useReducer

```
// File: src/components/CounterReducer.js
import React, { useReducer } from 'react';

// Define the initial state
const initialState = { count: 0 };
```

```jsx
// Define a reducer function
const counterReducer = (state, action) => {
  switch (action.type) {
    case 'increment':
      return { count: state.count + 1 };
    case 'decrement':
      return { count: state.count - 1 };
    default:
      return state;
  }
};

const CounterReducer = () => {
  const [state, dispatch] = useReducer(counterReducer,
initialState);

  return (
    <div style={{ textAlign: 'center', marginTop: '2rem'
}}>
      <h2>Count: {state.count}</h2>
      <button onClick={() => dispatch({ type: 'increment'
})} style={{ marginRight: '0.5rem' }}>
        Increase
      </button>
      <button onClick={() => dispatch({ type: 'decrement'
})}>
        Decrease
      </button>
    </div>
  );
};

export default CounterReducer;
```

Explanation:

- The `counterReducer` handles state transitions based on action types.
- `useReducer` returns the current state and a dispatch function to trigger state updates.
- Dispatching an action (e.g., `{ type: 'increment' }`) updates the state accordingly.

Personal Insight:
I've found `useReducer` especially useful for managing state in more complex forms and multi-step processes. Its structure encourages you to

think in terms of state transitions, making debugging and testing much more manageable.

6.4: Leveraging React Admin's Built-In State Patterns

React Admin is designed to streamline common tasks in admin dashboards, including state management. It provides built-in hooks and patterns that simplify handling data fetching, notifications, and refreshing views.

Key Features:

- **useNotify:** Easily display notifications for user actions.
- **useRefresh:** Programmatically refresh data on the dashboard.
- **useDataProvider:** Interact with the backend API in a consistent manner.

Practical Example: Using useNotify and useRefresh

Imagine you have a form submission that requires a notification and a data refresh. Here's how you can do it:

```
// File: src/components/CustomSaveButton.js
import React from 'react';
import { useNotify, useRefresh } from 'react-admin';
import Button from '@mui/material/Button';

const CustomSaveButton = ({ onSave }) => {
  const notify = useNotify();
  const refresh = useRefresh();

  const handleSave = async () => {
    try {
      await onSave(); // Assume onSave is a function that
saves data
      notify('Data saved successfully!', { type: 'success'
});
      refresh();
    } catch (error) {
      notify('Error saving data', { type: 'warning' });
```

```
      }
  };

  return (
    <Button variant="contained" color="primary"
onClick={handleSave}>
      Save Changes
    </Button>
  );
};

export default CustomSaveButton;
```

Explanation:

- **useNotify:** Displays success or error messages based on the outcome of a save operation.
- **useRefresh:** Triggers a refresh of the data, ensuring the latest information is displayed after updates.

Personal Insight:
Integrating these built-in hooks allowed me to focus on business logic rather than boilerplate code. They ensure consistency in user feedback and data management across the entire admin interface.

Intermediate state management techniques provide the tools you need to handle more complex data flows in React applications. By mastering local state with Hooks, sharing state with the Context API, implementing advanced logic with useReducer, and leveraging React Admin's built-in state patterns, you can build robust and maintainable admin dashboards.

These patterns not only enhance code clarity and maintainability but also empower you to build interactive and responsive applications. Experiment with the examples provided, tailor them to your project's needs, and enjoy the process of crafting sophisticated state management solutions.

Part III: Advanced Development and Optimization

Chapter 7: Performance Optimization Strategies

When building modern React applications, performance is key to ensuring a smooth user experience. In this chapter, we'll explore several strategies to optimize your React app. We'll start by understanding how React's rendering cycle works, then discuss how to prevent unnecessary re-renders with React.memo, optimize updates with useCallback and useMemo, implement code splitting and lazy loading, and finally, tackle the challenges of rendering large datasets through virtualization.

7.1: Understanding React's Rendering Cycle

React's rendering cycle is at the core of how your application updates its user interface. By understanding this cycle, you can make smarter decisions about optimizing your app's performance and avoiding unnecessary re-renders. In this guide, we'll walk through what happens under the hood when your components update, using clear explanations and practical examples to illustrate each step.

The Basics of React's Rendering Cycle

At its heart, React's rendering cycle is all about reconciling changes. When a component's state or props change, React re-executes the component function, generating a new Virtual DOM. It then compares this new Virtual DOM with the previous one—a process called "diffing"—to determine the minimal set of changes needed to update the real DOM.

Key Stages in the Cycle:

1. **Triggering a Re-render:**

- o A change in state, props, or context signals React to re-render a component.
- o Event handlers (like button clicks) often trigger these updates.

2. **Re-execution of the Component:**
   - o The component function is called again, and it returns a new Virtual DOM tree.
   - o This tree is a lightweight, in-memory representation of your UI.

3. **Reconciliation (Diffing):**
   - o React compares the new Virtual DOM tree with the previous one.
   - o It calculates the differences (or "diff") and determines which parts of the actual DOM need to be updated.

4. **DOM Updates:**
   - o Only the parts of the DOM that have changed are updated.
   - o This minimizes costly DOM operations and boosts performance.

Personal Insight:
I remember the first time I dove into React's rendering process—it was like opening a black box where I could see how minimal changes resulted in highly efficient updates. Understanding this cycle helped me appreciate why even small optimizations can make a big difference.

Practical Implementation: Logging Component Renders

To see React's rendering cycle in action, we can create a simple component that logs every time it renders. This will help illustrate when and why re-renders occur.

Step 1: Create a Render Logger Component

```
// File: src/components/RenderLogger.js
import React, { useEffect } from 'react';

const RenderLogger = ({ text }) => {
  useEffect(() => {
```

```
    console.log(`Rendered: ${text}`);
  });

  return <div>{text}</div>;
};

export default RenderLogger;
```

Explanation:

- **useEffect Hook:**
  The effect runs after every render, logging the current text.
- **Purpose:**
  This helps us track how often the component renders and can be a useful debugging tool.

Step 2: Integrate RenderLogger into a Parent Component

```
// File: src/components/ParentComponent.js
import React, { useState } from 'react';
import RenderLogger from './RenderLogger';

const ParentComponent = () => {
  const [count, setCount] = useState(0);

  return (
    <div style={{ textAlign: 'center', marginTop: '2rem'
}}>
      <button onClick={() => setCount(prev => prev + 1)}>
        Increment Count
      </button>
      <RenderLogger text={`Count: ${count}`} />
    </div>
  );
};

export default ParentComponent;
```

Explanation:

- **State Update:**
  Clicking the button increments the `count` state.
- **Render Observation:**
  Each time `count` changes, `ParentComponent` and its child `RenderLogger` re-render, and you'll see a log in the console.

Using this simple logging technique, I was able to pinpoint where unexpected re-renders were happening in my applications, which is often the first step in optimizing performance.

Diving Deeper: Batch Updates and the Diffing Algorithm

Batch Updates

React batches multiple state updates occurring within the same event loop to reduce the number of re-renders. For example, if you call multiple state updates in an event handler, React will process them together in one re-render, rather than one after the other.

The Diffing Algorithm

React's diffing algorithm (or reconciliation process) efficiently calculates changes by comparing the new and previous Virtual DOM trees. It uses heuristics to minimize the work done:

- **Key Prop:**
  When rendering lists, the `key` prop is essential for helping React identify which items have changed.
- **Component Hierarchy:**
  React compares component trees top-down, so a change high in the tree can trigger many child re-renders unless optimized.

Personal Insight:
I've often seen the benefits of proper key management in lists. A well-chosen key can significantly speed up the diffing process, reducing unnecessary DOM updates and improving overall performance.

Understanding React's rendering cycle is crucial for any developer looking to optimize their application's performance. By knowing how state changes trigger re-renders, how the Virtual DOM and diffing algorithm work, and by utilizing practical tools like logging renders, you can gain deep insights into your app's behavior.

7.2: Preventing Unnecessary Re-renders with React.memo

When building complex React applications, minimizing unnecessary re-renders can significantly boost performance. One powerful tool for this purpose is `React.memo`, a higher-order component that memoizes functional components. In this guide, we'll dive deep into how `React.memo` works, when to use it, and how it helps you prevent redundant renders. We'll also illustrate these concepts with practical, step-by-step examples.

What is React.memo?

`React.memo` is a higher-order component that wraps a functional component and memoizes its rendered output. This means that if the component's props have not changed, React can skip re-rendering the component, thus saving computational resources.

Key Points:

- **Memoization:**
  It caches the result of the component's render based on its props.
- **Pure Components:**
  `React.memo` works best for components that render the same output for the same props.
- **Usage:**
  It's particularly useful for components that are heavy to render or are part of large lists.

Personal Insight:
When I first started optimizing my React apps, I was astonished at the performance gains from simply wrapping components with `React.memo`.

It helped eliminate many unnecessary renders, especially in scenarios where complex lists or charts were involved.

How React.memo Works

Under the hood, `React.memo` performs a shallow comparison of the component's props. If the props remain unchanged, React skips the render of that component and reuses the previous result. This process is similar to how `PureComponent` works in class components.

Step-by-Step Example: Memoizing a Component

Example Scenario: An Expensive Component

Suppose we have a component that performs a complex calculation or renders a large list. We can wrap it with `React.memo` to avoid re-rendering unless its props change.

Step 1: Create a Basic Component
```
// File: src/components/ExpensiveComponent.js
import React from 'react';

const ExpensiveComponent = ({ value }) => {
  console.log("ExpensiveComponent rendered");
  // Imagine this component has heavy rendering logic
  return <div>Computed Value: {value}</div>;
};

export default ExpensiveComponent;
```
Step 2: Wrap the Component with React.memo
```
// File: src/components/MemoizedExpensiveComponent.js
import React from 'react';
import ExpensiveComponent from './ExpensiveComponent';

// Wrap the component with React.memo to prevent
unnecessary re-renders
```

```
const MemoizedExpensiveComponent =
React.memo(ExpensiveComponent);

export default MemoizedExpensiveComponent;
```

Explanation:

- **Console Logging:**
  The log "ExpensiveComponent rendered" will help us observe when the component is actually re-rendered.
- **Memoization:**
  With `React.memo`, if the `value` prop remains unchanged between renders, the component won't re-render.

Step 3: Use the Memoized Component in a Parent Component
```
// File: src/components/ParentComponent.js
import React, { useState } from 'react';
import MemoizedExpensiveComponent from
'./MemoizedExpensiveComponent';

const ParentComponent = () => {
  const [count, setCount] = useState(0);

  // The value prop is static, so
MemoizedExpensiveComponent should not re-render when count
changes
  return (
    <div style={{ textAlign: 'center', marginTop: '2rem'
}}>
      <button onClick={() => setCount(prev => prev + 1)}>
        Increment Count: {count}
      </button>
      <MemoizedExpensiveComponent value="Static Data" />
    </div>
  );
};

export default ParentComponent;
```

Explanation:

- **State Change:**
  The parent component has a `count` state that updates when the button is clicked.
- **Static Prop:**
  The `value` prop passed to `MemoizedExpensiveComponent` remains

"Static Data" every time. With `React.memo`, the expensive component does not re-render unnecessarily when `count` changes.

- **Observing Behavior:**
  Open the browser's console. You should notice that "ExpensiveComponent rendered" is logged only once, even if you click the button multiple times.

When to Use React.memo

Suitable Scenarios:

- **Heavy Components:**
  Components that perform complex calculations or render large amounts of data.
- **Pure Functional Components:**
  Components that consistently render the same output for the same set of props.
- **Optimizing Lists:**
  When rendering lists with many items, wrapping each list item component with `React.memo` can help improve performance.

Potential Pitfalls:

- **Shallow Comparison:**
  `React.memo` does a shallow comparison of props. If your props are objects or arrays that are recreated on every render, it might not prevent re-renders as expected. In such cases, consider using custom comparison functions as a second argument to `React.memo`.
- `const MemoizedComponent = React.memo(Component, (prevProps, nextProps) => {`
- `// Custom comparison logic`
- `return JSON.stringify(prevProps.data) === JSON.stringify(nextProps.data);`
- `});`
- **Over-Optimization:**
  Using `React.memo` indiscriminately can add complexity without significant benefits. It's best applied to components known to cause performance issues.

I once wrapped nearly every component in my app with `React.memo` in an attempt to optimize performance, only to realize that unnecessary memoization can complicate your codebase. Over time, I learned to identify the critical components where optimization matters most and apply `React.memo` selectively.

7.3: Utilizing useCallback and useMemo for Efficient Updates

When building dynamic React applications, performance can often hinge on how efficiently your components update. Two essential hooks—**useCallback** and **useMemo**—help you fine-tune these updates by avoiding unnecessary recalculations and function recreations. In this guide, we'll explore these hooks in detail, discuss when and why to use them, and walk through practical, step-by-step examples to illustrate their benefits.

Why useCallback and useMemo?

- **useCallback** helps you memoize functions, ensuring that the same instance of a function is reused between renders unless its dependencies change. This is particularly useful when passing callbacks to child components that might otherwise re-render unnecessarily.
- **useMemo** memoizes the result of an expensive computation so that it's recalculated only when its dependencies change. This can save you from running heavy operations on every render.

Personal Insight:
I remember the first time I encountered performance issues with my React app. Simple functions were being recreated on every render, and heavy computations were executed repeatedly. Incorporating useCallback and useMemo into my code not only improved performance but also made the code easier to reason about. They are like performance enhancers for your components.

Step-by-Step Example: Optimizing an Expensive Calculation and a Callback

Let's build a component that demonstrates both hooks. We'll create a component that computes the factorial of a number (an expensive operation) and includes a button to increment a counter. We'll use useMemo to avoid recalculating the factorial unnecessarily and useCallback to stabilize the increment function.

1. Define an Expensive Calculation Function

We'll start with a simple recursive function to compute the factorial of a number.

```
// File: src/utils/factorial.js
export const factorial = (n) => {
  console.log('Calculating factorial for', n);
  if (n <= 1) return 1;
  return n * factorial(n - 1);
};
```

Note: The console log helps us see when the calculation is triggered.

2. Create the Optimized Component

Now, let's build a component that uses both useMemo and useCallback.

```
// File: src/components/EfficientUpdatesComponent.js
import React, { useState, useMemo, useCallback } from
'react';
import { factorial } from '../utils/factorial';

// A child button component that only re-renders if its
props change
const ChildButton = React.memo(({ onIncrement }) => {
  console.log('ChildButton rendered');
  return <button onClick={onIncrement}>Increment
Count</button>;
});

const EfficientUpdatesComponent = () => {
  // State for the number used in the expensive calculation
```

```
  const [number, setNumber] = useState(5);
  // State for an unrelated counter
  const [count, setCount] = useState(0);

  // Memoize the factorial calculation: re-compute only
when 'number' changes
  const fact = useMemo(() => factorial(number), [number]);

  // Memoize the increment function: use a functional
update to avoid dependency on 'count'
  const incrementCount = useCallback(() => {
    setCount((prevCount) => prevCount + 1);
  }, []); // No dependencies since we use the functional
update form

  return (
    <div style={{ textAlign: 'center', marginTop: '2rem'
}}>
      <h2>Efficient Updates Component</h2>
      <div>
        <p>
          Factorial of {number} is: <strong>{fact}</strong>
        </p>
        <button onClick={() => setNumber((prev) => prev +
1)} style={{ marginRight: '1rem' }}>
          Increment Number
        </button>
      </div>
      <div style={{ marginTop: '2rem' }}>
        <p>
          Count: <strong>{count}</strong>
        </p>
        <ChildButton onIncrement={incrementCount} />
      </div>
    </div>
  );
};

export default EfficientUpdatesComponent;
```

Explanation of the Code:

- **useMemo for Expensive Calculations:**
- `const fact = useMemo(() => factorial(number), [number]);`

    This line ensures that the factorial is only recalculated when the number state changes. Even if other parts of the component re-

render, the expensive calculation is skipped if `number` remains the same.

- **useCallback for Stable Functions:**

```
const incrementCount = useCallback(() => {
  setCount((prevCount) => prevCount + 1);
}, []);
```

Here, useCallback memoizes the `incrementCount` function so that its identity remains stable across renders. This is particularly useful for the `ChildButton` component wrapped with `React.memo`, as it prevents unnecessary re-renders due to a new function reference on every render.

- **React.memo with Child Components:**
  The `ChildButton` component is wrapped with `React.memo`, so it only re-renders when its props change. Because `incrementCount` is stable (thanks to useCallback), `ChildButton` won't re-render unless truly needed.

Personal Insight:
Before using these hooks, my app would frequently re-render components that didn't need to update, which was both inefficient and confusing during debugging. Introducing useMemo and useCallback helped me pinpoint when expensive computations or function recreations were happening, leading to a more responsive and maintainable codebase.

When to Use useCallback and useMemo

- **useCallback:**
  - When you need to pass a callback to a memoized child component.
  - When a function is recreated unnecessarily on each render and causes performance issues.
- **useMemo:**
  - When you have an expensive calculation that you don't want to run on every render.

o   When you need to memoize the result of a computation that depends on certain variables.

Tip:
Always profile your application before and after introducing these optimizations. Overusing them without need can sometimes add unnecessary complexity.

7.4: Implementing Code Splitting and Lazy Loading

As your React application grows, loading the entire codebase upfront can lead to slow initial load times and a poor user experience. Code splitting and lazy loading help mitigate this issue by breaking your code into smaller chunks that are loaded on demand. In this guide, we'll explore these techniques, explain how they work, and walk through practical, step-by-step examples to implement them in your React projects.

Why Code Splitting and Lazy Loading?

Code Splitting refers to breaking down your application into smaller bundles rather than one large file. This way, users load only the code necessary for the current view, speeding up initial load times.

Lazy Loading complements this by loading components or modules only when they are needed. This means that parts of your application that are not immediately required can be fetched asynchronously, reducing the amount of JavaScript the browser needs to process during startup.

Personal Insight:
I remember the first time I implemented code splitting in a project—it was a revelation. Suddenly, the app felt snappier, and users no longer had to wait for a monolithic bundle to load. It taught me the importance of optimizing for performance, especially as projects scale.

Step-by-Step Implementation

Step 1: Setting Up Your Environment

Make sure you are using a recent version of React (v16.6 or later), as React.lazy and Suspense were introduced in this release.

Step 2: Using React.lazy for Component Lazy Loading

React provides the `React.lazy()` function to enable dynamic import of components. This allows you to split code at the component level.

Example: Lazy Loading a Component

1. Create a Component to Lazy Load

Let's assume we have a component that is heavy or rarely used, for example, a Dashboard Details component.

```
// File: src/components/DashboardDetails.js
import React from 'react';

const DashboardDetails = () => {
  return (
    <div>
      <h2>Dashboard Details</h2>
      <p>This component contains detailed statistics and
charts.</p>
      {/* Imagine there are heavy charts or data
visualizations here */}
    </div>
  );
};

export default DashboardDetails;
```

2. Lazy Load the Component in Your Main App

Next, import this component lazily using `React.lazy` and wrap its usage in a `Suspense` component to provide a fallback UI while it loads.

```
// File: src/App.js
import React, { Suspense, lazy } from 'react';
```

```
const DashboardDetails = lazy(() =>
import('./components/DashboardDetails'));

const App = () => {
  return (
    <div>
      <h1>My React App</h1>
      <Suspense fallback={<div>Loading Dashboard
Details...</div>}>
        <DashboardDetails />
      </Suspense>
    </div>
  );
};

export default App;
```

Explanation:

- **React.lazy:**
  The `lazy()` function takes a function that returns a dynamic import. This tells React to load the component only when it's rendered.
- **Suspense:**
  This component wraps the lazy-loaded component and provides a fallback UI (like a loading spinner or message) until the component is fully loaded.

Step 3: Code Splitting with Dynamic Imports

Beyond components, you can also dynamically import other parts of your code such as utility functions or modules when they're needed.

Example: Dynamically Importing a Utility Function

Imagine you have a utility that performs complex calculations. You might not need it immediately on the initial render.

```
// File: src/utils/heavyCalculation.js
export const heavyCalculation = (num) => {
  // Imagine a heavy, CPU-intensive calculation here
  let result = 1;
  for (let i = 1; i <= num; i++) {
```

```
      result *= i;
  }
  return result;
};
```

Now, use dynamic import to load this function when needed:

```
// File: src/components/CalculationComponent.js
import React, { useState } from 'react';

const CalculationComponent = () => {
  const [result, setResult] = useState(null);

  const handleCalculate = async () => {
    const { heavyCalculation } = await
import('../utils/heavyCalculation');
    const calcResult = heavyCalculation(10);
    setResult(calcResult);
  };

  return (
    <div style={{ textAlign: 'center', marginTop: '2rem'
}}>
      <button onClick={handleCalculate}>Calculate Factorial
of 10</button>
      {result && <p>Result: {result}</p>}
    </div>
  );
};

export default CalculationComponent;
```

Explanation:

- **Dynamic Import:**
  The `import('../utils/heavyCalculation')` is a dynamic import that loads the module when `handleCalculate` is invoked. This keeps the heavy calculation code out of the main bundle.
- **Async/Await:**
  Using async/await syntax allows you to handle the dynamic import as a promise, making the code clean and readable.

Personal Insight:
In one of my projects, the initial load was painfully slow because a rarely-used but heavy module was included in the main bundle. By dynamically

importing that module, the load time improved significantly, and users only downloaded the extra code when they needed it.

Step 4: Combining Code Splitting with Routing

React Router integrates well with lazy loading, allowing you to code split at the route level. This means each route can load its components on demand.

Example: Code Splitting with React Router

1. **Install React Router (if not already installed):**

```
npm install react-router-dom
```

2. **Set Up Routes with Lazy Loaded Components:**

```javascript
// File: src/App.js
import React, { Suspense, lazy } from 'react';
import { BrowserRouter as Router, Routes, Route, Link }
from 'react-router-dom';

const Home = lazy(() => import('./components/Home'));
const About = lazy(() => import('./components/About'));

const App = () => {
  return (
    <Router>
      <nav style={{ padding: '1rem', backgroundColor:
'#ddd' }}>
        <Link to="/" style={{ marginRight: '1rem'
}}>Home</Link>
        <Link to="/about">About</Link>
      </nav>
      <Suspense fallback={<div>Loading...</div>}>
        <Routes>
          <Route path="/" element={<Home />} />
          <Route path="/about" element={<About />} />
        </Routes>
      </Suspense>
    </Router>
  );
};
```

```
export default App;
```

Explanation:

- **Routes & Suspense:**
  Routes are wrapped within `Suspense` so that if any lazy-loaded route component is still being fetched, the fallback UI is shown.
- **Dynamic Component Loading:**
  Both the Home and About components are loaded only when the route is accessed.

Personal Insight:
Integrating lazy loading with routing was a turning point in optimizing my applications. It allows for a more efficient use of network resources and ensures that users only download the code necessary for the view they are interacting with.

7.5: Virtualization Techniques for Large Data Sets

When your application needs to display thousands of items—be it a long list, table, or grid—rendering all of them at once can lead to performance issues. Virtualization is a technique that addresses this challenge by rendering only the items visible in the viewport, plus a small buffer, rather than the entire list. In this guide, we'll explore the concept of virtualization, discuss popular libraries like **react-window** and **react-virtualized**, and walk through a step-by-step implementation using a practical code example.

What is Virtualization?

Virtualization (or windowing) is a performance optimization technique where only a small subset of data is rendered at any given time. This is particularly useful for large datasets because it minimizes the number of DOM nodes, reducing rendering time and improving responsiveness.

Key Benefits:

- **Improved Performance:**
  By rendering only visible items, your application uses less memory and executes faster.
- **Smooth Scrolling:**
  Users experience seamless scrolling even with thousands of items.
- **Reduced Browser Load:**
  Limits the computational overhead by not rendering off-screen elements.

Personal Insight:
I once had a dashboard that needed to display over 5,000 records in a table. The app was sluggish and unresponsive. Switching to virtualization techniques dramatically improved performance, making the interface smooth and efficient.

Popular Libraries for Virtualization

1. react-window

- **Lightweight:** Designed for simplicity and minimal overhead.
- **Flexible:** Provides components for fixed-size and variable-size lists and grids.
- **Ease of Use:** Simple API with excellent performance for most use cases.

2. react-virtualized

- **Feature-Rich:** Offers more advanced features like cell measurers, infinite loaders, and more.
- **Customizable:** Suitable for complex scenarios where you need more control over virtualization.
- **Steeper Learning Curve:** More configuration options, which might be overkill for simple lists.

For most applications, **react-window** strikes a good balance between performance and ease of use.

Step-by-Step Implementation with react-window

We'll create a simple virtualized list that displays 1,000 items. This example demonstrates how to use **react-window** to render only the items in view.

Step 1: Install react-window

Open your terminal in your project directory and run:

```
npm install react-window
```

Step 2: Create a Virtualized List Component

Create a file named `VirtualizedList.js` in your `src/components` directory:

```
// File: src/components/VirtualizedList.js
import React from 'react';
import { FixedSizeList as List } from 'react-window';

// A simple row component that renders each item
const Row = ({ index, style }) => (
  <div style={{ ...style, display: 'flex', alignItems:
'center', padding: '0 1rem', borderBottom: '1px solid #eee'
}}>
    Row {index + 1}
  </div>
);

const VirtualizedList = () => {
  const itemCount = 1000;   // Total number of items
  const itemHeight = 35;    // Height of each row in pixels
  const listHeight = 300;   // Height of the list container
in pixels

  return (
    <div style={{ margin: '2rem auto', width: '80%' }}>
      <h2 style={{ textAlign: 'center' }}>Virtualized List
Example</h2>
      <List
        height={listHeight}
```

```
        itemCount={itemCount}
        itemSize={itemHeight}
        width="100%"
      >
        {Row}
      </List>
    </div>
  );
};

export default VirtualizedList;
```

Explanation:

- **FixedSizeList:**
  This component from **react-window** is used when each item in the list has a fixed height. It takes properties such as `height`, `itemCount`, `itemSize`, and `width`.
- **Row Component:**
  The `Row` component renders each item. It receives `index` (to know which item to display) and `style` (which is crucial for positioning the item correctly). The style prop is automatically provided by **react-window** and must be attached to the row element.
- **Container Styling:**
  The outer `<div>` centers the list on the page and provides a title.

Step 3: Integrate the Virtualized List into Your Application

Modify your main application file to include the `VirtualizedList` component:

```
// File: src/App.js
import React from 'react';
import VirtualizedList from './components/VirtualizedList';

const App = () => {
  return (
    <div>
      <VirtualizedList />
    </div>
  );
};

export default App;
```

Additional Considerations

Handling Variable Item Sizes

If your items do not have a fixed height, **react-window** also provides a `VariableSizeList` component. You will need to supply a function that returns the height of each item.

Combining with Infinite Scrolling

For dynamic data, consider integrating virtualization with an infinite loader to fetch more data as the user scrolls. Both **react-window** and **react-virtualized** support these patterns.

Performance Profiling

Always use browser developer tools and profiling techniques to measure the impact of virtualization on your application. Virtualization should significantly reduce the number of DOM nodes, but testing on real devices ensures the best user experience.

Personal Insight:
In one of my projects, virtualization reduced the rendered DOM nodes from over 5,000 to just a fraction at any time. This resulted in smoother scrolling and an overall snappier application, proving that sometimes the best optimization is simply not rendering what the user isn't seeing.

Virtualization is an essential technique for optimizing performance in React applications that handle large data sets. By using libraries like **react-window**, you can significantly reduce the rendering workload by only displaying what's visible on the screen. The step-by-step example provided demonstrates how to implement a basic virtualized list, which you can further adapt to more complex scenarios.

Embrace virtualization to keep your applications responsive, reduce memory usage, and provide a smoother experience for users. Experiment with these techniques, and watch your app's performance improve as it scales.

Chapter 8: Complex State Handling and Global State Management

As your applications grow in complexity, managing state across many components becomes a challenge. Local state management with Hooks works well for simpler scenarios, but larger apps often require a robust global state solution. In this chapter, we'll explore various global state management options, how to integrate Redux with React Admin, strategies for handling asynchronous data with Redux Thunk and Redux Saga, and techniques for normalizing and debugging your state.

Personal Insight:
I've experienced firsthand the struggles of state management in large applications. Moving from local state to a centralized solution like Redux not only improved the maintainability of my projects but also made debugging and scaling much more manageable.

8.1: Evaluating Global State Solutions: Redux and Alternatives

In modern React applications, managing state across many components can become challenging as the application grows. Global state management solutions offer a way to maintain a single source of truth, making your code more predictable and easier to debug. In this section, we'll take an in-depth look at Redux—one of the most popular global state management libraries—and briefly compare it with some alternatives. We'll discuss their strengths and weaknesses and provide practical examples to help you decide which solution best fits your project.

Redux: The Battle-Tested Champion

Overview

Redux is a predictable state container that follows a unidirectional data flow. It centralizes your state in a single store and uses pure functions (reducers) to update that state based on dispatched actions.

Pros

- **Predictability:** With a single source of truth and immutable state updates, Redux makes it easier to track changes.
- **Extensive Ecosystem:** Redux offers a wealth of middleware (like Redux Thunk and Redux Saga), dev tools, and community support.
- **Debuggability:** Time-travel debugging and detailed logs with Redux DevTools help pinpoint issues quickly.

Cons

- **Boilerplate Code:** Redux requires setting up actions, reducers, and sometimes middleware, which can feel verbose, especially in small projects.
- **Learning Curve:** The concepts of immutability, middleware, and the Redux pattern can be challenging for newcomers.

Practical Implementation: A Simple Redux Setup

1. **Install Redux and React-Redux:**

```
npm install redux react-redux
```

2. **Create a Redux Store and Reducer:**

```
// File: src/store.js
import { createStore, combineReducers, applyMiddleware }
from 'redux';
import thunk from 'redux-thunk';

// Example: A simple authentication reducer
const authReducer = (state = { isAuthenticated: false,
user: null }, action) => {
  switch (action.type) {
    case 'LOGIN_SUCCESS':
      return { ...state, isAuthenticated: true, user:
action.payload };
```

```
    case 'LOGOUT':
      return { ...state, isAuthenticated: false, user: null
};
    default:
      return state;
  }
};

// Combine reducers if you have more than one
const rootReducer = combineReducers({
  auth: authReducer,
  // Add other reducers here
});

// Create the store with middleware (e.g., Redux Thunk for
async actions)
const store = createStore(rootReducer,
applyMiddleware(thunk));

export default store;
```

3. **Provide the Store to Your Application:**

```
// File: src/index.js
import React from 'react';
import ReactDOM from 'react-dom';
import { Provider } from 'react-redux';
import App from './App';
import store from './store';

ReactDOM.render(
  <React.StrictMode>
    <Provider store={store}>
      <App />
    </Provider>
  </React.StrictMode>,
  document.getElementById('root')
);
```

4. **Connect a Component to Redux:**

```
// File: src/components/CustomHeader.js
import React from 'react';
import { useSelector } from 'react-redux';
import { AppBar, Toolbar, Typography } from
'@mui/material';

const CustomHeader = () => {
  const user = useSelector((state) => state.auth.user);
```

```
  return (
    <AppBar position="static">
      <Toolbar>
        <Typography variant="h6">
          {user ? `Welcome, ${user.name}` : 'React Admin
Dashboard'}
        </Typography>
      </Toolbar>
    </AppBar>
  );
};

export default CustomHeader;
```

Personal Insight:
Integrating Redux into my projects provided a clear structure for handling complex state logic. The Redux DevTools were invaluable during debugging, and once you get past the initial boilerplate, the predictability of state changes pays dividends in larger applications.

Alternatives to Redux

While Redux is a powerful and widely adopted solution, it might be overkill for smaller projects or teams looking for a simpler approach. Here are a few alternatives:

MobX

- **Pros:**
  - o Uses observable state, making it very reactive.
  - o Less boilerplate compared to Redux.
- **Cons:**
  - o Can lead to less predictable state management if not used carefully.
  - o Some developers prefer the explicitness of Redux's unidirectional data flow.

Recoil

- **Pros:**

- o Developed by Facebook, Recoil is designed to work seamlessly with React.
- o Offers fine-grained control over state with atoms and selectors.
- **Cons:**
  - o It's relatively new and has a smaller community compared to Redux.
  - o API is still evolving, which might introduce breaking changes.

Zustand

- **Pros:**
  - o Minimalistic and very simple to use.
  - o Offers a flexible API with minimal boilerplate.
- **Cons:**
  - o Lacks the extensive middleware ecosystem that Redux provides.
  - o Best suited for smaller or medium-sized applications.

Expert Commentary:
The choice of a global state solution often depends on the size and complexity of your application. Redux is a solid choice for large-scale projects where predictability and maintainability are paramount. However, if you're building something smaller or prefer a less verbose setup, exploring alternatives like MobX, Recoil, or Zustand might be beneficial.

8.2: Integrating Redux with React Admin

When building large-scale applications, managing global state becomes crucial, and Redux has long been a popular solution. React Admin, while powerful on its own, sometimes benefits from Redux's centralized state management—especially for tasks like handling authentication, user settings, or global notifications. In this guide, we'll walk through integrating Redux with React Admin in a detailed, step-by-step approach, complete with practical code examples and insights drawn from real-world experience.

Why Integrate Redux with React Admin?

React Admin is designed to handle many administrative tasks, including data fetching, resource management, and UI rendering. However, certain aspects—like handling authentication, managing global notifications, or synchronizing application-wide settings—are better managed through a global state solution like Redux. This integration allows you to:

- **Centralize Global State:**
  Keep track of shared state (e.g., current user, permissions) in one place.
- **Improve Debugging:**
  Use tools like Redux DevTools to monitor state changes.
- **Enhance Scalability:**
  Easily manage complex state interactions as your application grows.

Personal Insight:
Integrating Redux into my React Admin projects was a turning point. Initially, I struggled with scattered state logic, but centralizing it in Redux made the application much more predictable and easier to debug, especially when dealing with asynchronous user actions.

Step 1: Setting Up Redux

Before integrating Redux with React Admin, ensure Redux and React-Redux are installed in your project.

Installation

Run the following command in your project directory:

```
npm install redux react-redux redux-thunk
```

- **redux:** The core Redux library.
- **react-redux:** The official bindings for React.
- **redux-thunk:** Middleware for handling asynchronous actions (optional, but commonly used).

Creating a Redux Store

Create a file named store.js in your src directory. This file will configure your Redux store and combine your reducers.

```
// File: src/store.js
import { createStore, combineReducers, applyMiddleware }
from 'redux';
import thunk from 'redux-thunk';

// Example reducer: manages authentication state
const authReducer = (state = { isAuthenticated: false,
user: null }, action) => {
  switch (action.type) {
    case 'LOGIN_SUCCESS':
      return { ...state, isAuthenticated: true, user:
action.payload };
    case 'LOGOUT':
      return { ...state, isAuthenticated: false, user: null
};
    default:
      return state;
  }
};

// You can add additional reducers here
const rootReducer = combineReducers({
  auth: authReducer,
  // Add other reducers as needed
});

// Create the Redux store with middleware (using redux-
thunk for async actions)
const store = createStore(rootReducer,
applyMiddleware(thunk));

export default store;
```

Explanation:

- We define a simple authentication reducer that handles login and logout actions.
- The reducers are combined into a single root reducer.
- The store is created with the combined reducer and middleware, making it ready for integration.

Personal Insight:
I found that starting with a simple, well-structured store helps in gradually scaling your Redux logic as your application requirements expand.

Step 2: Connecting Redux to Your React Admin App

Now that the Redux store is set up, the next step is to connect it to your React Admin application using the Redux Provider.

Wrapping Your App with the Redux Provider

Modify your `src/index.js` file to include the Redux Provider.

```
// File: src/index.js
import React from 'react';
import ReactDOM from 'react-dom';
import { Provider } from 'react-redux';
import App from './App';
import store from './store';

ReactDOM.render(
  <React.StrictMode>
    <Provider store={store}>
      <App />
    </Provider>
  </React.StrictMode>,
  document.getElementById('root')
);
```

Explanation:

- The `Provider` component from `react-redux` makes the Redux store available to all components in your application.
- By wrapping your entire app with `Provider`, you ensure that any component can access the global state using hooks like `useSelector` and `useDispatch`.

Step 3: Integrating Redux with React Admin

React Admin's `<Admin>` component is the core of your admin dashboard. You can integrate Redux into React Admin by connecting your custom components (like headers, sidebars, or custom actions) to the Redux store.

Example: Custom Header with User Information

Create a custom header component that reads authentication data from Redux and displays a welcome message.

```
// File: src/components/CustomHeader.js
import React from 'react';
import { useSelector } from 'react-redux';
import { AppBar, Toolbar, Typography } from
'@mui/material';

const CustomHeader = () => {
  // Use the useSelector hook to extract the user from the
Redux state
  const user = useSelector((state) => state.auth.user);

  return (
    <AppBar position="static">
      <Toolbar>
        <Typography variant="h6">
          {user ? `Welcome, ${user.name}` : 'React Admin
Dashboard'}
        </Typography>
      </Toolbar>
    </AppBar>
  );
};

export default CustomHeader;
```

Explanation:

- **useSelector Hook:** This hook accesses the Redux store's state and retrieves the current user information.
- **Material-UI Components:** Used to create a professional-looking header.

Personal Insight:
Integrating Redux with React Admin through custom components allowed me to tailor the user experience. Displaying dynamic data like user

information directly from the global state made the app feel more cohesive and responsive to user actions.

Incorporating Custom Components into React Admin

Now, integrate your custom header into your React Admin layout. Modify your App.js file as follows:

```
// File: src/App.js
import React from 'react';
import { Admin, Resource } from 'react-admin';
import jsonServerProvider from 'ra-data-json-server';
import CustomHeader from './components/CustomHeader';
import PostList from './posts/PostList';
import PostCreate from './posts/PostCreate';
import PostEdit from './posts/PostEdit';
import PostShow from './posts/PostShow';

const dataProvider =
jsonServerProvider('https://jsonplaceholder.typicode.com');

const App = () => (
  <Admin dataProvider={dataProvider} appBar={CustomHeader}>
    <Resource
      name="posts"
      list={PostList}
      create={PostCreate}
      edit={PostEdit}
      show={PostShow}
    />
  </Admin>
);

export default App;
```

Explanation:

- The appBar prop on the <Admin> component is used to replace the default header with your custom Redux-connected header.
- This integration demonstrates how Redux can augment React Admin's functionality without disrupting its core features.

Integrating Redux with React Admin provides a robust solution for managing global state in your administrative applications. By setting up a Redux store, connecting it with the Redux Provider, and creating custom components that leverage global state, you can enhance your application's

140

functionality—especially for features like authentication, notifications, and user preferences.

8.3: Managing Asynchronous Data with Redux Thunk and Redux Saga

Managing asynchronous operations—like fetching data from an API—is a common challenge in modern applications. In Redux, handling these asynchronous actions can be elegantly managed using middleware. Two of the most popular middleware solutions are **Redux Thunk** and **Redux Saga**. In this guide, we'll explore both, discuss when and why to use them, and walk through detailed, step-by-step code examples to demonstrate their practical implementations.

Why Handle Asynchronous Data?

In a Redux application, actions are typically synchronous by default. However, real-world applications often need to perform tasks such as:

- Fetching data from remote servers
- Submitting forms
- Handling user authentication
- Processing real-time updates

Without middleware, you'd need to manage these asynchronous flows outside of Redux, making your state management fragmented and harder to debug. Middleware like Redux Thunk and Redux Saga helps encapsulate async logic within your Redux actions and flows.

Redux Thunk

Overview

Redux Thunk is a middleware that allows you to write action creators that return a function instead of an action object. This function receives the `dispatch` and `getState` methods as arguments, which lets you perform asynchronous tasks and dispatch actions when they complete.

Pros and Cons

- **Pros:**
    - **Simplicity:** Easy to set up and use for most straightforward async operations.
    - **Direct Integration:** Works seamlessly with Redux; you can write async logic directly in your action creators.
    - **Less Boilerplate:** Minimal additional code compared to more complex solutions.
- **Cons:**
    - **Complexity in Large Applications:** As your app grows, managing many async operations with Thunk can become harder to maintain.
    - **Limited Abstraction:** It does not provide built-in tools for handling more complex workflows like cancellation or concurrency.

Practical Example: Fetching Data with Redux Thunk

Step 1: Install Redux Thunk

```
npm install redux-thunk
```

Step 2: Configure Redux Store with Thunk Middleware

```
// File: src/store.js
import { createStore, combineReducers, applyMiddleware }
from 'redux';
import thunk from 'redux-thunk';

// Example data reducer for handling API calls
const dataReducer = (state = { items: [], loading: false,
error: null }, action) => {
  switch (action.type) {
    case 'DATA_FETCH_REQUEST':
      return { ...state, loading: true, error: null };
    case 'DATA_FETCH_SUCCESS':
      return { ...state, loading: false, items:
action.payload };
    case 'DATA_FETCH_FAILURE':
      return { ...state, loading: false, error:
action.error };
```

```
    default:
      return state;
  }
};

const rootReducer = combineReducers({
  data: dataReducer,
  // Include other reducers here
});

const store = createStore(rootReducer,
applyMiddleware(thunk));

export default store;
```

Step 3: Create an Asynchronous Action Creator with Thunk
```
// File: src/actions/dataActions.js
export const fetchData = () => async (dispatch) => {
  dispatch({ type: 'DATA_FETCH_REQUEST' });
  try {
    const response = await
fetch('https://jsonplaceholder.typicode.com/posts');
    const data = await response.json();
    dispatch({ type: 'DATA_FETCH_SUCCESS', payload: data
});
  } catch (error) {
    dispatch({ type: 'DATA_FETCH_FAILURE', error:
error.message });
  }
};
```

Step 4: Use the Async Action in a Component
```
// File: src/components/DataList.js
import React, { useEffect } from 'react';
import { useDispatch, useSelector } from 'react-redux';
import { fetchData } from '../actions/dataActions';

const DataList = () => {
  const dispatch = useDispatch();
  const { items, loading, error } = useSelector((state) =>
state.data);

  useEffect(() => {
    dispatch(fetchData());
  }, [dispatch]);

  if (loading) return <p>Loading data...</p>;
  if (error) return <p>Error: {error}</p>;

  return (
    <ul>
      {items.map((item) => (
```

```
      <li key={item.id}>{item.title}</li>
    )))}
  </ul>
  );
};

export default DataList;
```

Personal Insight:
Using Redux Thunk allowed me to handle API calls directly within my action creators. It streamlined the process and kept my asynchronous logic neatly encapsulated, making it much easier to track state changes related to data fetching.

Redux Saga

Overview

Redux Saga leverages ES6 generator functions to handle side effects in a more declarative way. Instead of writing inline async logic, you define sagas—separate functions that listen for actions and then perform asynchronous tasks. This approach provides a clear separation between the action flow and side effect logic.

Pros and Cons

- **Pros:**
    - **Powerful Control Flow:** Easily manage complex asynchronous workflows, including cancellation and concurrency.
    - **Declarative Side Effects:** Sagas make your side effect logic more explicit and easier to follow.
    - **Testability:** Generator functions are simpler to test as you can step through them.
- **Cons:**
    - **Steeper Learning Curve:** Understanding generators and saga effects requires additional learning.
    - **More Boilerplate:** Setting up sagas can be more verbose compared to Thunk for simple tasks.

Practical Example: Fetching Data with Redux Saga

Step 1: Install Redux Saga

```
npm install redux-saga
```

Step 2: Create a Saga for Data Fetching

```javascript
// File: src/sagas/dataSaga.js
import { call, put, takeLatest } from 'redux-saga/effects';

// Function to fetch data
const fetchDataFromApi = () => {
  return
fetch('https://jsonplaceholder.typicode.com/posts').then((r
esponse) => response.json());
};

function* fetchDataSaga() {
  try {
    yield put({ type: 'DATA_FETCH_REQUEST' });
    const data = yield call(fetchDataFromApi);
    yield put({ type: 'DATA_FETCH_SUCCESS', payload: data
});
  } catch (error) {
    yield put({ type: 'DATA_FETCH_FAILURE', error:
error.message });
  }
}

export function* watchFetchData() {
  yield takeLatest('TRIGGER_DATA_FETCH', fetchDataSaga);
}
```

Step 3: Integrate Redux Saga into the Store

```javascript
// File: src/store.js
import { createStore, combineReducers, applyMiddleware }
from 'redux';
import createSagaMiddleware from 'redux-saga';
import { watchFetchData } from './sagas/dataSaga';

// Data reducer (same as before)
const dataReducer = (state = { items: [], loading: false,
error: null }, action) => {
  switch (action.type) {
    case 'DATA_FETCH_REQUEST':
      return { ...state, loading: true, error: null };
    case 'DATA_FETCH_SUCCESS':
      return { ...state, loading: false, items:
action.payload };
    case 'DATA_FETCH_FAILURE':
      return { ...state, loading: false, error:
action.error };
```

```
      default:
        return state;
  }
};

const rootReducer = combineReducers({
  data: dataReducer,
  // Other reducers...
});

const sagaMiddleware = createSagaMiddleware();

const store = createStore(rootReducer,
applyMiddleware(sagaMiddleware));

sagaMiddleware.run(watchFetchData);

export default store;
```

Step 4: Trigger the Saga from a Component

```
// File: src/components/DataListSaga.js
import React, { useEffect } from 'react';
import { useDispatch, useSelector } from 'react-redux';

const DataListSaga = () => {
  const dispatch = useDispatch();
  const { items, loading, error } = useSelector((state) =>
state.data);

  useEffect(() => {
    // Dispatch an action that triggers the saga
    dispatch({ type: 'TRIGGER_DATA_FETCH' });
  }, [dispatch]);

  if (loading) return <p>Loading data...</p>;
  if (error) return <p>Error: {error}</p>;

  return (
    <ul>
      {items.map((item) => (
        <li key={item.id}>{item.title}</li>
      ))}
    </ul>
  );
};

export default DataListSaga;
```

Personal Insight:
While Redux Saga introduces more boilerplate than Thunk, I found it

146

incredibly useful for managing complex async workflows, especially in scenarios involving multiple API calls or when actions need to be canceled or run concurrently. Sagas give a clear, declarative approach that scales well with complexity.

When to Choose Redux Thunk vs. Redux Saga

- **Redux Thunk:**
    o Best for simpler asynchronous tasks.
    o Lower overhead and easier to understand for straightforward API calls.
- **Redux Saga:**
    o Ideal for complex scenarios where you need fine-grained control over side effects.
    o Better for managing sequences of actions, cancellations, and complex asynchronous flows.

Personal Insight:
I tend to use Redux Thunk for most small to medium projects because of its simplicity. However, for large-scale applications with intricate data flows or where performance and cancellation are critical, Redux Saga has proven to be a more robust and maintainable choice.

8.4: Techniques for State Normalization and Debugging

In larger applications, state management can quickly become a tangled web of duplicated data and complex update logic. State normalization is a powerful technique to organize your data much like a relational database—storing entities in a way that avoids redundancy and makes updates predictable and efficient. In this chapter, we'll dive into how to normalize your state, why it's beneficial, and share debugging techniques that can help you keep track of state changes and identify issues quickly. We'll also walk through practical, step-by-step examples to illustrate these concepts.

What is State Normalization?

State normalization involves structuring your data so that each entity is stored in a lookup table (or object) keyed by a unique identifier (such as an ID), along with an array of IDs that represent the order of these entities. This mirrors the relational database approach, where you avoid duplicating data and maintain a single source of truth for each entity.

Benefits of Normalization

- **Avoid Redundancy:**
  By storing each entity once, updates are simpler and less error-prone.
- **Efficient Updates:**
  When you need to update an entity, you only update it in one place.
- **Improved Debugging:**
  A normalized state is easier to inspect using tools like Redux DevTools because the data structure is predictable and organized.

Personal Insight:
I once struggled with a component that rendered a list of posts, each containing nested comments. Whenever a comment updated, I had to traverse multiple arrays and objects. Normalizing the data simplified the update logic dramatically, and it made debugging a breeze with Redux DevTools.

Step-by-Step: Normalizing State in Redux

Let's take a practical example. Imagine you're fetching a list of posts from an API. Instead of storing the posts in an array, we can normalize the state by storing posts in an object keyed by their IDs, along with an array of IDs to preserve order.

Step 1: Setting Up the Normalized State Structure

Create an initial state that looks like this:

```
// File: src/reducers/postsReducer.js

const initialState = {
  posts: {},    // Object to store posts by ID
  postIds: []   // Array to store the order of post IDs
};

const postsReducer = (state = initialState, action) => {
  switch (action.type) {
    case 'SET_POSTS':
      // Assume action.payload is an array of posts
      const postsArray = action.payload;
      const normalizedPosts = {};
      const postIds = [];

      postsArray.forEach(post => {
        normalizedPosts[post.id] = post;
        postIds.push(post.id);
      });

      return { ...state, posts: normalizedPosts, postIds };

    case 'UPDATE_POST':
      // action.payload contains { id, changes }
      const { id, changes } = action.payload;
      return {
        ...state,
        posts: { ...state.posts, [id]: {
...state.posts[id], ...changes } }
      };

    default:
      return state;
  }
};

export default postsReducer;
```

Explanation:

- **SET_POSTS:**
  When fetching posts from an API, we normalize the array into an
  object (normalizedPosts) and maintain an array of IDs
  (postIds).
- **UPDATE_POST:**
  Updates a specific post by merging its current data with new
  changes.

Step 2: Dispatching Actions

To populate the state, dispatch an action that sets the posts:

```
// File: src/actions/postsActions.js
export const setPosts = (posts) => ({
  type: 'SET_POSTS',
  payload: posts
});

export const updatePost = (id, changes) => ({
  type: 'UPDATE_POST',
  payload: { id, changes }
});
```

You can then fetch data from your API and dispatch these actions accordingly.

Debugging Techniques

Even with normalized state, debugging complex applications can be challenging. Here are some effective techniques:

1. Redux DevTools

Redux DevTools is an essential tool that lets you inspect every action, state transition, and even perform time-travel debugging. Make sure to integrate it into your Redux store setup:

```
// File: src/store.js
import { createStore, combineReducers, applyMiddleware,
compose } from 'redux';
import thunk from 'redux-thunk';
import postsReducer from './reducers/postsReducer';

const rootReducer = combineReducers({
  posts: postsReducer,
  // ...other reducers
});

// Enable Redux DevTools Extension if available
const composeEnhancers =
window.__REDUX_DEVTOOLS_EXTENSION_COMPOSE__ || compose;
```

```
const store = createStore(rootReducer,
composeEnhancers(applyMiddleware(thunk)));

export default store;
```

2. Logging Middleware

Sometimes, a simple console log can reveal a lot about the state changes.
You can add custom middleware to log actions and state:

```
// File: src/middleware/logger.js
const logger = store => next => action => {
  console.log('Dispatching:', action);
  const result = next(action);
  console.log('Next state:', store.getState());
  return result;
};

export default logger;
```

Integrate it into your store configuration:

```
// File: src/store.js (update middleware)
import logger from './middleware/logger';
const store = createStore(rootReducer,
composeEnhancers(applyMiddleware(thunk, logger)));
```

3. Normalizr Library

For complex nested data, consider using normalizr to automate the
normalization process.

Example:
```
// File: src/utils/normalizeData.js
import { normalize, schema } from 'normalizr';

// Define a post schema
const post = new schema.Entity('posts');
const postListSchema = [post];

export const normalizePosts = (data) => normalize(data,
postListSchema);
```

Then, when fetching data:

```
import { normalizePosts } from '../utils/normalizeData';

const fetchPosts = async () => {
  const response = await
fetch('https://jsonplaceholder.typicode.com/posts');
  const data = await response.json();
  const normalizedData = normalizePosts(data);
  // Dispatch action with normalizedData.entities.posts and
normalizedData.result
};
```

Personal Insight:
Using libraries like normalizr not only reduces boilerplate but also enforces a consistent structure in your state. I've found that once you adopt normalization, debugging state updates becomes much simpler—each entity is stored in one place, so you can quickly trace changes and fix issues.

State normalization and effective debugging are cornerstones of scalable Redux applications. Normalizing state minimizes redundancy and streamlines updates, while tools like Redux DevTools, custom logging middleware, and libraries like normalizr provide robust mechanisms to inspect and troubleshoot your state.

Part IV: Specialized Backend Integration and Advanced Features

Chapter 9: Advanced API Integration

In advanced React Admin applications, integrating with backends goes far beyond basic CRUD operations. This chapter explores advanced API integration techniques that empower you to build robust, real-time, and fault-tolerant admin interfaces. We'll cover how data providers work, how to build custom data providers for both REST and GraphQL APIs, methods for handling errors, caching, and optimistic updates, and finally, how to integrate real-time data through WebSockets and Server-Sent Events (SSE).

Personal Insight:
Throughout my projects, I've learned that a well-designed API integration layer not only simplifies data management but also dramatically improves the user experience. With these advanced techniques, you can make your admin dashboard responsive, resilient, and even real-time—delivering the kind of polished experience that users appreciate.

9.1: Understanding Data Providers in React Admin

Data providers are the backbone of React Admin's ability to interact with your backend. They serve as an abstraction layer that translates the declarative queries from your UI into concrete API calls. In this guide, we'll explore what data providers are, how they work, and why they're essential for building a scalable admin dashboard. We'll also walk through practical, step-by-step code examples to illustrate these concepts, sharing personal insights along the way.

What Is a Data Provider?

In React Admin, a data provider is an object or function that implements a standard interface to handle all data operations. Instead of scattering API calls throughout your components, React Admin centralizes data fetching, updating, and error handling in the data provider. This abstraction makes it easy to swap out your backend without changing your UI logic.

Key Responsibilities

- **Mapping CRUD Operations:**
  A data provider translates React Admin actions like GET_LIST, GET_ONE, CREATE, UPDATE, and DELETE into API requests.
- **Handling Data Transformation:**
  It formats the data received from the backend into the shape expected by React Admin, and vice versa.
- **Error Management:**
  The data provider can catch and process errors, ensuring your UI can respond appropriately.

Personal Insight:
When I first learned about data providers, it was a revelation. Having a single layer to manage API interactions not only made my code cleaner but also allowed for easier debugging and testing. It's like having a universal translator between your UI and backend.

The Standard Data Provider Interface

React Admin expects your data provider to implement a set of methods corresponding to common operations:

- **getList:** Retrieves a list of records.
- **getOne:** Fetches a single record by ID.
- **getMany:** Retrieves multiple records by an array of IDs.
- **create:** Sends a new record to the backend.
- **update:** Modifies an existing record.
- **delete:** Removes a record.
- **getManyReference:** Fetches records related to another resource.

Each method typically returns a promise that resolves to an object with the requested data.

Using a Built-In Data Provider: JSON Server Example

React Admin offers several pre-built data providers. One popular choice for demos and prototyping is `ra-data-json-server`, which works with JSON Server APIs.

Step 1: Installation

Open your terminal in your project directory and run:

```
npm install ra-data-json-server
```

Step 2: Integrate the Data Provider into Your App

Here's a simple example using the JSONPlaceholder API:

```
// File: src/App.js
import React from 'react';
import { Admin, Resource } from 'react-admin';
import jsonServerProvider from 'ra-data-json-server';
import PostList from './posts/PostList';

// Configure the data provider with the demo API endpoint
const dataProvider =
jsonServerProvider('https://jsonplaceholder.typicode.com');

const App = () => (
  <Admin dataProvider={dataProvider}>
    <Resource name="posts" list={PostList} />
  </Admin>
);

export default App;
```

Step 3: Creating a Simple List View

```
// File: src/posts/PostList.js
import React from 'react';
import { List, Datagrid, TextField } from 'react-admin';

const PostList = () => (
```

```
  <List>
    <Datagrid rowClick="edit">
      <TextField source="id" label="ID" />
      <TextField source="title" label="Title" />
      <TextField source="body" label="Content" />
    </Datagrid>
  </List>
);

export default PostList;
```

Explanation:

- The data provider sends HTTP requests to the JSONPlaceholder API.
- The `<Resource>` component registers the "posts" resource, mapping CRUD operations to the corresponding endpoints.
- The `PostList` view displays data in a tabular format, automatically benefiting from the data provider's implementation.

Building a Custom Data Provider

Sometimes you need more control than a pre-built provider can offer—for example, to add custom headers, transform data, or work with non-standard APIs. In these cases, you can build your own data provider.

Step 1: Define Your Custom Data Provider

Below is an example for a REST API:

```
// File: src/dataProvider.js
const apiUrl = 'https://api.example.com';

const customDataProvider = {
  getList: (resource, params) => {
    const { page, perPage } = params.pagination;
    const query = new URLSearchParams({
      _page: page,
      _limit: perPage,
      _sort: params.sort.field,
      _order: params.sort.order,
    });
```

```
        return
fetch(`${apiUrl}/${resource}?${query.toString()}`)
      .then(response => {
        const total = parseInt(response.headers.get('X-
Total-Count'), 10);
        return response.json().then(data => ({ data, total
}));
      })
      .catch(error => {
        console.error('Error fetching list:', error);
        throw error;
      });
  },

  getOne: (resource, params) =>
    fetch(`${apiUrl}/${resource}/${params.id}`)
      .then(response => response.json())
      .then(data => ({ data })),

  create: (resource, params) =>
    fetch(`${apiUrl}/${resource}`, {
      method: 'POST',
      headers: { 'Content-Type': 'application/json' },
      body: JSON.stringify(params.data),
    })
      .then(response => response.json())
      .then(data => ({ data })),

  update: (resource, params) =>
    fetch(`${apiUrl}/${resource}/${params.id}`, {
      method: 'PUT',
      headers: { 'Content-Type': 'application/json' },
      body: JSON.stringify(params.data),
    })
      .then(response => response.json())
      .then(data => ({ data })),

  delete: (resource, params) =>
    fetch(`${apiUrl}/${resource}/${params.id}`, { method:
'DELETE' })
      .then(response => response.json())
      .then(data => ({ data })),
};

export default customDataProvider;
```

Step 2: Use Your Custom Data Provider

Integrate your custom data provider into your React Admin app:

```
// File: src/App.js
import React from 'react';
import { Admin, Resource } from 'react-admin';
import customDataProvider from './dataProvider';
import PostList from './posts/PostList';

const App = () => (
  <Admin dataProvider={customDataProvider}>
    <Resource name="posts" list={PostList} />
  </Admin>
);

export default App;
```

Explanation:

- Each method in the custom data provider corresponds to a React Admin action.
- The provider uses the native `fetch` API to make HTTP requests.
- Errors are caught and logged to help with debugging.

Personal Insight:
Building a custom data provider was challenging at first, but once I understood the required interface, it gave me tremendous flexibility. I could tailor API calls to my specific backend, add authentication headers, or even transform the data before passing it to my UI—all without changing the structure of my React Admin components.

Data providers are a critical piece of React Admin, acting as the bridge between your user interface and your backend. By using pre-built providers like `ra-data-json-server`, you can quickly prototype and deploy admin interfaces. However, for more complex or customized scenarios, building your own data provider gives you the control you need over API calls, error handling, and data transformation.

9.2: Building Custom Data Providers for REST and GraphQL

In React Admin, a data provider serves as the bridge between your admin interface and your backend API. While pre-built data providers are available for common backends, building a custom data provider gives you full control over how data is fetched, transformed, and error-handled. In this guide, we'll explore how to build custom data providers for both REST and GraphQL APIs. We'll walk through detailed, step-by-step examples and share insights to help you tailor the integration to your application's needs.

Why Build a Custom Data Provider?

Custom data providers let you:

- **Tailor API Calls:** Add custom headers (like authentication tokens), handle specific query parameters, or transform data formats.
- **Improve Error Handling:** Implement robust error management strategies that suit your backend.
- **Unify Data Flow:** Maintain consistency across different API types (REST vs. GraphQL) without altering your UI components.

Personal Insight:
When I first ventured into custom data providers, I was amazed at how decoupling the API logic from the UI not only simplified maintenance but also made my application more resilient to backend changes. This separation of concerns is a key principle in building scalable applications.

Building a Custom REST Data Provider

A REST data provider translates React Admin's CRUD queries into HTTP requests. Here's how you can build one step by step.

Step 1: Define the API URL

Set up a constant for your API endpoint. For demonstration purposes, we'll use a placeholder URL.

```
// File: src/dataProviderREST.js
const apiUrl = 'https://api.example.com';
```

Step 2: Implement CRUD Methods

Implement methods like `getList`, `getOne`, `create`, `update`, and `delete`. Each method should return a promise that resolves with the data in the format expected by React Admin.

```
// File: src/dataProviderREST.js
const customRESTDataProvider = {
  getList: (resource, params) => {
    const { page, perPage } = params.pagination;
    const { field, order } = params.sort;
    // Build query parameters for pagination and sorting
    const query = new URLSearchParams({
      _page: page,
      _limit: perPage,
      _sort: field,
      _order: order,
    });
    return
fetch(`${apiUrl}/${resource}?${query.toString()}`)
      .then(response => {
        // Extract total count from headers if provided
        const total = parseInt(response.headers.get('X-
Total-Count'), 10);
        return response.json().then(data => ({ data, total
}));
      })
      .catch(error => {
        console.error(`Error in getList for resource
${resource}:`, error);
        throw error;
      });
  },

  getOne: (resource, params) =>
    fetch(`${apiUrl}/${resource}/${params.id}`)
      .then(response => response.json())
      .then(data => ({ data })),

  create: (resource, params) =>
    fetch(`${apiUrl}/${resource}`, {
      method: 'POST',
      headers: { 'Content-Type': 'application/json' },
      body: JSON.stringify(params.data),
    })
      .then(response => response.json())
      .then(data => ({ data })),

  update: (resource, params) =>
```

```
      fetch(`${apiUrl}/${resource}/${params.id}`, {
        method: 'PUT',
        headers: { 'Content-Type': 'application/json' },
        body: JSON.stringify(params.data),
      })
        .then(response => response.json())
        .then(data => ({ data })),

  delete: (resource, params) =>
    fetch(`${apiUrl}/${resource}/${params.id}`, {
      method: 'DELETE',
    })
      .then(response => response.json())
      .then(data => ({ data })),
};

export default customRESTDataProvider;
```

Step 3: Integrate the REST Data Provider with React Admin

Now that the REST data provider is ready, plug it into your React Admin application:

```
// File: src/App.js
import React from 'react';
import { Admin, Resource } from 'react-admin';
import customRESTDataProvider from './dataProviderREST';
import PostList from './posts/PostList';
import PostEdit from './posts/PostEdit';
import PostCreate from './posts/PostCreate';
import PostShow from './posts/PostShow';

const App = () => (
  <Admin dataProvider={customRESTDataProvider}>
    <Resource
      name="posts"
      list={PostList}
      edit={PostEdit}
      create={PostCreate}
      show={PostShow}
    />
  </Admin>
);

export default App;
```

Explanation:

- Each method of the custom REST provider handles specific CRUD operations.
- React Admin uses these methods to automatically generate routes and manage data.

Building a Custom GraphQL Data Provider

GraphQL requires a different approach, as it involves sending queries and mutations instead of standard HTTP verbs. Let's build a simplified GraphQL data provider using Apollo Client.

Step 1: Set Up Apollo Client

Install Apollo Client and its dependencies:

```
npm install @apollo/client graphql
```

Configure Apollo Client in your project:

```
// File: src/apolloClient.js
import { ApolloClient, InMemoryCache } from
'@apollo/client';

const client = new ApolloClient({
  uri: 'https://graphql.example.com',
  cache: new InMemoryCache(),
});

export default client;
```

Step 2: Create the GraphQL Data Provider

Implement methods that send GraphQL queries and mutations using Apollo Client.

```
// File: src/dataProviderGraphQL.js
import client from './apolloClient';
import { gql } from '@apollo/client';

const customGraphQLDataProvider = {
  getList: async (resource, params) => {
    const { page, perPage } = params.pagination;
```

```
    const { field, order } = params.sort;

    // Define a GraphQL query (customize this query as per
your schema)
    const GET_LIST = gql`
       query GetList($page: Int!, $perPage: Int!,
$sortField: String!, $sortOrder: String!) {
         ${resource}(page: $page, perPage: $perPage,
sortField: $sortField, sortOrder: $sortOrder) {
            data {
              id
              title
              content
            }
            total
          }
        }
      `;

    const { data } = await client.query({
      query: GET_LIST,
      variables: { page, perPage, sortField: field,
sortOrder: order },
    });
    return { data: data[resource].data, total:
data[resource].total };
  },

  getOne: async (resource, params) => {
    const GET_ONE = gql`
      query GetOne($id: ID!) {
        ${resource}(id: $id) {
          id
          title
          content
        }
      }
    `;
    const { data } = await client.query({
      query: GET_ONE,
      variables: { id: params.id },
    });
    return { data: data[resource] };
  },

  // Implement create, update, delete similarly using
mutations
};

export default customGraphQLDataProvider;
```

Step 3: Integrate the GraphQL Data Provider

Use the custom GraphQL data provider in your React Admin application just like any other provider:

```
// File: src/App.js
import React from 'react';
import { Admin, Resource } from 'react-admin';
import customGraphQLDataProvider from
'./dataProviderGraphQL';
import PostList from './posts/PostList';
import PostEdit from './posts/PostEdit';
import PostCreate from './posts/PostCreate';
import PostShow from './posts/PostShow';

const App = () => (
  <Admin dataProvider={customGraphQLDataProvider}>
    <Resource
      name="posts"
      list={PostList}
      edit={PostEdit}
      create={PostCreate}
      show={PostShow}
    />
  </Admin>
);

export default App;
```

Explanation:

- The GraphQL data provider sends queries and mutations via Apollo Client.
- It transforms GraphQL responses into the format expected by React Admin.

Personal Insight:
Building a custom GraphQL data provider initially seemed complex, but it provided the flexibility to interact with a modern API. It allows you to write queries that exactly match your backend schema, making the integration seamless and powerful.

Custom data providers are a cornerstone of building advanced React Admin applications. They allow you to tailor API interactions to your exact requirements—whether you're working with a traditional REST API or a modern GraphQL endpoint.

Key Takeaways:

- **Custom REST Provider:**
  Implement CRUD methods using standard HTTP requests and transform responses to meet React Admin's expectations.
- **Custom GraphQL Provider:**
  Use Apollo Client to send queries and mutations, adapting GraphQL responses for React Admin.
- **Flexibility and Control:**
  Custom providers give you the ability to handle authentication headers, error management, and data transformation in a centralized way.

By mastering custom data providers, you'll be able to integrate virtually any backend with React Admin, paving the way for highly customized and scalable admin dashboards.

9.3: Error Handling, Caching, and Optimistic Updates

When integrating your admin interface with backend APIs, handling errors gracefully, caching data effectively, and providing immediate feedback through optimistic updates are essential techniques. These strategies improve user experience, reduce latency, and make your application more resilient to network issues. In this guide, we'll dive into each of these concepts with in-depth analysis, expert commentary, and step-by-step, practical code examples.

Personal Insight:
In my experience, robust error handling and caching not only enhance reliability but also foster user trust. Optimistic updates, when done correctly, provide immediate feedback, making your application feel snappy—even if the backend takes a little longer to respond.

Error Handling

Why Error Handling Matters

Proper error handling ensures that your application can gracefully manage unexpected issues such as network failures, server errors, or malformed data. Instead of crashing or leaving the user in the dark, effective error handling displays informative messages and, when possible, allows users to retry actions.

Step-by-Step: Implementing Error Handling in a Custom Data Provider

Let's enhance a custom REST data provider to handle errors.

Example: Enhanced `getList` Method with Error Handling

```
// File: src/dataProviderREST.js
const apiUrl = 'https://api.example.com';

const customRESTDataProvider = {
  getList: (resource, params) => {
    const { page, perPage } = params.pagination;
    const { field, order } = params.sort;
    const query = new URLSearchParams({
      _page: page,
      _limit: perPage,
      _sort: field,
      _order: order,
    });

    return
fetch(`${apiUrl}/${resource}?${query.toString()}`)
      .then(response => {
        if (!response.ok) {
          return response.text().then(text => {
            throw new Error(text || 'Error fetching data');
          });
        }
        const total = parseInt(response.headers.get('X-
Total-Count'), 10);
        return response.json().then(data => ({ data, total
})));
      })
      .catch(error => {
        console.error(`Error in getList for resource
"${resource}":`, error);
```

```
      throw error;
    });
  },

  // ... other CRUD methods (getOne, create, update,
delete) with similar error handling
};

export default customRESTDataProvider;
```

Explanation:

- **Response Validation:**
  The code checks if the response is OK. If not, it extracts the error message (or uses a default message) and throws an error.
- **Error Logging:**
  Logging the error to the console aids in debugging.
- **Error Propagation:**
  By throwing errors, the data provider allows React Admin (or your components) to catch and handle these issues, perhaps by displaying a notification.

Caching

The Role of Caching

Caching minimizes the number of network requests by storing previously fetched data locally. This not only improves performance but also reduces the load on your backend. Effective caching can lead to faster load times and a smoother user experience.

Step-by-Step: Implementing Basic Caching

Below is a simplified caching strategy for a getOne method.

Example: Simple Caching in a Data Provider
```
// File: src/dataProviderWithCache.js
const apiUrl = 'https://api.example.com';
const cache = {};

const dataProviderWithCache = {
```

```
getOne: (resource, params) => {
  const cacheKey = `${resource}_${params.id}`;
  if (cache[cacheKey]) {
    return Promise.resolve({ data: cache[cacheKey] });
  }
  return fetch(`${apiUrl}/${resource}/${params.id}`)
    .then(response => {
      if (!response.ok) {
        throw new Error(`Error fetching resource
${resource} with id ${params.id}`);
      }
      return response.json();
    })
    .then(data => {
      cache[cacheKey] = data;
      return { data };
    });
},

// Implement other methods with caching logic as
needed...
};

export default dataProviderWithCache;
```

Explanation:

- **Cache Key Generation:**
  The cache key is created based on the resource and ID.
- **Cache Check:**
  Before making a network request, the method checks if the data is already cached.
- **Storing Data:**
  Fetched data is stored in the cache for subsequent requests.

Personal Insight:
I've seen significant performance improvements in applications where caching was implemented correctly. Even a simple in-memory cache can drastically reduce redundant API calls for data that doesn't change often.

Optimistic Updates

What Are Optimistic Updates?

Optimistic updates provide immediate UI feedback by assuming that a change will succeed, updating the state before the server confirms the change. If the operation fails, the update is rolled back. This approach can greatly enhance perceived performance.

Step-by-Step: Implementing Optimistic Updates in a Redux Action

Example: Optimistic Update in Redux

Suppose you have an action to update a post. The optimistic update will immediately reflect the changes in the UI, then confirm or rollback based on the API response.

```
// File: src/actions/postActions.js
export const updatePostOptimistic = (id, changes) =>
(dispatch, getState) => {
  // Get the current state for potential rollback
  const originalPost = getState().posts.posts[id];

  // Optimistically update the UI
  dispatch({ type: 'UPDATE_POST', payload: { id, changes }
});

  // Make the API call to update the post
  return fetch(`https://api.example.com/posts/${id}`, {
    method: 'PUT',
    headers: { 'Content-Type': 'application/json' },
    body: JSON.stringify(changes),
  })
    .then(response => {
      if (!response.ok) throw new Error('Update failed');
      return response.json();
    })
    .then(data => {
      // Optionally dispatch a success action or simply
leave the optimistic update
      dispatch({ type: 'UPDATE_POST_SUCCESS', payload: {
id, data } });
    })
    .catch(error => {
      // Roll back the optimistic update if the API call
fails
      dispatch({ type: 'UPDATE_POST', payload: { id,
changes: originalPost } });
      dispatch({ type: 'UPDATE_POST_FAILURE', payload: {
id, error: error.message } });
```

```
      console.error('Optimistic update failed:', error);
      throw error;
    });
};
```

Explanation:

- **Optimistic Dispatch:**
  Immediately update the state with the new changes.
- **API Call:**
  Perform the actual update via a network request.
- **Rollback Mechanism:**
  If the API call fails, dispatch an action to revert the changes to the
  original state.
- **User Feedback:**
  Optionally, dispatch success or failure actions to notify the user of
  the outcome.

Personal Insight:
Optimistic updates can make your application feel incredibly responsive. I
once implemented an optimistic update for a comment system, and users
were thrilled with how quickly their changes appeared. The key is robust
error handling—ensuring that if the backend fails, the UI gracefully
reverts to the correct state.

In this chapter, we've explored three critical techniques for managing API
interactions in advanced React Admin applications: error handling,
caching, and optimistic updates. By implementing robust error handling,
you ensure your application gracefully manages failures and
communicates issues to users. Caching reduces unnecessary network
requests and enhances performance, while optimistic updates provide a
responsive user experience by updating the UI immediately.

9.4: Integrating Real-Time Data with WebSockets and SSE

Real-time data can transform an admin dashboard into a dynamic,
responsive tool—providing live updates for notifications, metrics, or
collaborative data. In this guide, we'll explore how to integrate real-time

data into your React Admin application using two popular approaches: WebSockets and Server-Sent Events (SSE). We'll break down each technique, discuss their differences, and provide practical, step-by-step examples with complete, working code.

Personal Insight:
I've experienced the dramatic difference that real-time data can make. In one project, integrating WebSockets brought our dashboard to life, offering instantaneous updates that significantly improved user engagement and operational efficiency.

Understanding Real-Time Data Integration

Real-time data integration enables your application to receive updates from the server as soon as they occur, rather than relying solely on periodic polling. Two common methods for achieving this are:

- **WebSockets:**
  Provides full-duplex, bidirectional communication between the client and server, allowing both to send data at any time.
- **Server-Sent Events (SSE):**
  Allows the server to push updates to the client over a unidirectional channel. SSE is simpler for cases where only the server sends data.

Using WebSockets for Real-Time Data

WebSockets are ideal when you need bidirectional communication. They are well-suited for applications like chat apps, collaborative tools, or dashboards that need to both send and receive data.

Step 1: Create a WebSocket Client

First, create a simple WebSocket client that abstracts the connection logic.

```
// File: src/websocketClient.js
class WebSocketClient {
```

```
  constructor(url) {
    this.socket = new WebSocket(url);
  }

  // Register a callback for incoming messages
  onMessage(callback) {
    this.socket.onmessage = (event) => {
      const data = JSON.parse(event.data);
      callback(data);
    };
  }

  // Send data to the server
  send(data) {
    this.socket.send(JSON.stringify(data));
  }

  // Close the WebSocket connection
  close() {
    this.socket.close();
  }
}

export default WebSocketClient;
```

Step 2: Integrate WebSocket in a React Component

Use the WebSocket client in a component to receive and display real-time updates.

```
// File: src/components/RealTimeUpdates.js
import React, { useEffect, useState } from 'react';
import WebSocketClient from '../websocketClient';

const RealTimeUpdates = () => {
  const [updates, setUpdates] = useState([]);

  useEffect(() => {
    // Replace with your WebSocket server URL
    const client = new WebSocketClient('wss://your-
websocket-server-url');

    // Listen for incoming messages
    client.onMessage((data) => {
      setUpdates((prevUpdates) => [data, ...prevUpdates]);
    });

    // Cleanup on unmount
    return () => client.close();
```

```
  }, []);

  return (
    <div style={{ padding: '1rem' }}>
      <h3>Real-Time Updates (WebSocket)</h3>
      <ul>
        {updates.map((update, index) => (
          <li key={index}>{JSON.stringify(update)}</li>
        ))}
      </ul>
    </div>
  );
};

export default RealTimeUpdates;
```

Explanation:

- We instantiate the `WebSocketClient` with a server URL.
- The `onMessage` method sets up a listener that updates local state when a message is received.
- The component cleans up by closing the connection when unmounted.

Using Server-Sent Events (SSE) for Real-Time Data

SSE is a simpler, unidirectional method where the server pushes updates to the client over HTTP. It is a great choice when you only need to receive data from the server.

Step 1: Create an SSE Component

Set up a component that connects to an SSE endpoint.

```
// File: src/components/SSEUpdates.js
import React, { useEffect, useState } from 'react';

const SSEUpdates = () => {
  const [messages, setMessages] = useState([]);

  useEffect(() => {
```

```
    // Replace with your SSE endpoint URL
    const eventSource = new EventSource('https://your-sse-
endpoint');

    eventSource.onmessage = (event) => {
      const newMessage = JSON.parse(event.data);
      setMessages((prev) => [newMessage, ...prev]);
    };

    eventSource.onerror = (error) => {
      console.error('SSE error:', error);
      eventSource.close();
    };

    // Cleanup when component unmounts
    return () => {
      eventSource.close();
    };
  }, []);

  return (
    <div style={{ padding: '1rem' }}>
      <h3>Real-Time Updates (SSE)</h3>
      <ul>
        {messages.map((msg, idx) => (
          <li key={idx}>{JSON.stringify(msg)}</li>
        ))}
      </ul>
    </div>
  );
};

export default SSEUpdates;
```

Explanation:

- An `EventSource` object connects to the SSE endpoint.
- Incoming messages are parsed and added to local state.
- Error handling ensures the connection is closed if an error occurs.

Comparing WebSockets and SSE

- **WebSockets:**
  - o **Pros:**

- Bidirectional communication (both client and server can send messages).
- Suitable for interactive applications (e.g., chats, multiplayer games).
  - **Cons:**
    - Slightly more complex to set up and manage.
    - Requires handling connection lifecycles manually.
- **SSE:**
  - **Pros:**
    - Simpler for unidirectional data flow (server to client).
    - Native support in modern browsers with automatic reconnection.
  - **Cons:**
    - Only supports server-to-client communication.
    - Less efficient for highly interactive, bidirectional use cases.

Personal Insight:
For my projects, I typically use WebSockets when interactivity is key—like in chat systems—while SSE works wonderfully for dashboards where the server just needs to push periodic updates. Choosing the right tool depends on your specific requirements.

Integrating real-time data into your React Admin application can greatly enhance user engagement and operational responsiveness. Whether you choose WebSockets for full-duplex communication or SSE for a simpler server-to-client flow, both methods can be implemented effectively with a few lines of code.

Chapter 10: Implementing Advanced Authentication and Authorization

When it comes to building robust admin dashboards, securing your application is as important as its functionality. Advanced authentication and authorization ensure that only the right users can access sensitive data and perform critical actions. In this chapter, we'll explore how to implement advanced security measures, covering:

- **10.1: Building Custom Authentication Providers**
- **10.2: Managing Tokens: JWT, OAuth, and Session Strategies**
- **10.3: Implementing Role-Based Access Control (RBAC)**
- **10.4: Securing API Endpoints and Sensitive Data**

We'll walk through each section with clear, step-by-step examples and practical insights, making the concepts easy to understand and implement.

10.1: Building Custom Authentication Providers

Authentication is the gateway to a secure admin dashboard—it ensures that only authorized users can access sensitive data and features. While React Admin provides some default behavior, building a custom authentication provider allows you to tailor the login, logout, and authorization flows to your application's specific needs. In this guide, we'll explore what a custom authentication provider is, discuss its key methods, and walk through a detailed, step-by-step example to implement one.

What Is a Custom Authentication Provider?

A custom authentication provider in React Admin is an object that implements a set of methods to manage user authentication. Rather than scattering authentication logic throughout your app, you encapsulate it in a single provider. This not only promotes cleaner code but also makes your authentication strategy more predictable and easier to maintain.

Key Methods

A typical authentication provider includes the following methods:

- **login:** Handles user login, validates credentials, and stores authentication tokens.
- **logout:** Clears authentication data, effectively logging the user out.
- **checkAuth:** Checks whether the user is authenticated when navigating between pages.
- **checkError:** Handles errors related to authentication (e.g., token expiration).
- **getPermissions:** Retrieves the current user's roles or permissions for access control.

Step-by-Step: Building a Custom Authentication Provider

Below is a complete, working example of a custom authentication provider that uses the browser's localStorage to store a JWT (JSON Web Token) and user information.

Step 1: Define the Provider Structure

Create a file named `authProvider.js` in your `src` directory. This file will export an object with the necessary methods.

```
// File: src/authProvider.js

export default {
  // Called when the user attempts to log in
  login: ({ username, password }) => {
    // Replace with your real authentication API call
    return fetch('https://api.example.com/auth/login', {
```

```
      method: 'POST',
      headers: { 'Content-Type': 'application/json' },
      body: JSON.stringify({ username, password }),
    })
      .then((response) => {
        if (!response.ok) {
          // Throw an error if the response is not ok
          throw new Error('Invalid credentials');
        }
        return response.json();
      })
      .then(({ token, user }) => {
        // Save token and user info in localStorage for
persistence
        localStorage.setItem('authToken', token);
        localStorage.setItem('user', JSON.stringify(user));
      });

  },

  // Called when the user clicks on the logout button
  logout: () => {
    localStorage.removeItem('authToken');
    localStorage.removeItem('user');
    return Promise.resolve();
  },

  // Called to check if the user is authenticated
  checkAuth: () =>
    localStorage.getItem('authToken')
      ? Promise.resolve()
      : Promise.reject({ redirectTo: '/login' }),

  // Called when the API returns an authentication error
  checkError: (error) => {
    const status = error.status;
    if (status === 401 || status === 403) {
      localStorage.removeItem('authToken');
      localStorage.removeItem('user');
      return Promise.reject();
    }
    return Promise.resolve();
  },

  // Called to get the user's permissions (roles, etc.)
  getPermissions: () => {
    const user = localStorage.getItem('user');
    return user ? Promise.resolve(JSON.parse(user).roles) :
Promise.reject();
  },
```

```
};
```

Explanation:

- **login:**
  Sends a POST request to your authentication API with the user's credentials. On a successful response, it stores the returned token and user details in localStorage. This method returns a promise that either resolves (on success) or rejects (if credentials are invalid).
- **logout:**
  Clears authentication data by removing the token and user details from localStorage.
- **checkAuth:**
  Verifies the presence of an authentication token. If no token is found, it rejects the promise and optionally redirects the user to a login page.
- **checkError:**
  Processes errors from API calls. If an error status of 401 (Unauthorized) or 403 (Forbidden) is detected, it clears the stored authentication data and rejects the promise.
- **getPermissions:**
  Retrieves the user's roles or permissions from localStorage. This can be used to enforce role-based access control (RBAC) in your admin dashboard.

Personal Insight:
I found that creating a custom authentication provider helped me centralize all authentication-related logic. This approach made it much easier to manage token storage, error handling, and user permissions. It also simplified the process of integrating third-party authentication services later on.

Step 2: Integrate the Authentication Provider with React Admin

To use your custom authentication provider in your React Admin application, pass it as a prop to the <Admin> component.

```
// File: src/App.js
```

```
import React from 'react';
import { Admin, Resource } from 'react-admin';
import authProvider from './authProvider';
import dataProvider from './dataProvider'; // Your data
provider (could be REST or GraphQL)
import PostList from './posts/PostList';
import PostEdit from './posts/PostEdit';
import PostCreate from './posts/PostCreate';
import PostShow from './posts/PostShow';

const App = () => (
  <Admin dataProvider={dataProvider}
authProvider={authProvider}>
    <Resource
      name="posts"
      list={PostList}
      create={PostCreate}
      edit={PostEdit}
      show={PostShow}
    />
  </Admin>
);

export default App;
```

Explanation:

- The `authProvider` is injected into the React Admin `<Admin>` component, which then uses it to manage authentication flows.
- Your application can now automatically handle login, logout, and session validation based on the logic defined in your custom authentication provider.

Building a custom authentication provider in React Admin provides you with the flexibility to define how your application handles user authentication. By implementing the key methods—**login, logout, checkAuth, checkError**, and **getPermissions**—you can control the authentication process in a centralized and maintainable way.

10.2: Managing Tokens: JWT, OAuth, and Session Strategies

Managing tokens is essential for secure authentication and authorization in modern web applications. In this guide, we'll explore three common strategies for token management: **JWT (JSON Web Tokens)**, **OAuth**, and **Session-based** approaches. We'll break down how each works, discuss their strengths and trade-offs, and provide step-by-step, practical code examples to help you implement and manage tokens effectively.

Personal Insight:
Early in my career, I grappled with balancing security and usability when it came to authentication. Over time, I discovered that choosing the right token strategy isn't just about security—it's also about ensuring a smooth, responsive user experience. Let's dive in!

JWT (JSON Web Tokens)

Overview

JWTs are self-contained tokens that carry user information and expiration data. They are digitally signed, meaning the server can verify their authenticity without needing to maintain session state. This makes them popular for stateless authentication.

Key Features

- **Self-contained:** Includes claims like user roles and expiration.
- **Stateless:** The server doesn't need to store session data.
- **Portable:** Can be stored in localStorage, sessionStorage, or cookies.

Practical Implementation

When a user logs in, the server returns a JWT. You can store this token in localStorage for simplicity.

```
// File: src/auth/login.js
export const login = async ({ username, password }) => {
  const response = await
fetch('https://api.example.com/auth/login', {
    method: 'POST',
    headers: { 'Content-Type': 'application/json' },
    body: JSON.stringify({ username, password }),
  });

  if (!response.ok) {
    throw new Error('Invalid credentials');
  }

  const { token, user } = await response.json();
  localStorage.setItem('authToken', token);
  localStorage.setItem('user', JSON.stringify(user));
};
```

Decoding a JWT (Optional)

Sometimes, you may need to inspect the JWT to check expiration or extract user details. You can write a simple decoder or use a library like jwt-decode.

```
// File: src/utils/jwt.js
export const parseJwt = (token) => {
  try {
    const base64Url = token.split('.')[1];
    const base64 = base64Url.replace(/-/g,
'+').replace(/_/g, '/');
    const jsonPayload = decodeURIComponent(
      atob(base64)
        .split('')
        .map(c => '%' + ('00' +
c.charCodeAt(0).toString(16)).slice(-2))
        .join('')
    );
    return JSON.parse(jsonPayload);
  } catch (error) {
    console.error('Error parsing JWT:', error);
    return null;
  }
};
```

```
// Usage example
const token = localStorage.getItem('authToken');
const payload = parseJwt(token);
console.log('JWT Payload:', payload);
```

Personal Insight:
JWTs simplify authentication by eliminating server-side session storage, but they require careful handling—especially regarding token expiration and secure storage.

OAuth

Overview

OAuth is a framework for authorization that lets users grant limited access to their resources on one site to another without sharing their credentials. It's commonly used for third-party authentication (e.g., logging in with Google or Facebook).

How OAuth Works

1. **Authorization Request:** The user is redirected to the OAuth provider.
2. **User Consent:** The user approves the access request.
3. **Token Exchange:** The client receives an authorization code and exchanges it for an access token.
4. **Access Resources:** The client uses the token to access protected resources.

Practical Implementation

Initiating the OAuth Flow
```
// File: src/oauth.js
export const initiateOAuth = () => {
  const redirectUri =
encodeURIComponent(window.location.origin +
'/auth/callback');
  window.location.href =
`https://oauth.example.com/authorize?client_id=YOUR_CLIENT_
ID&redirect_uri=${redirectUri}&response_type=code&scope=rea
d:posts`;
```

```
};
```

After the user authorizes the application, they are redirected back with an authorization code. You then exchange this code for an access token.

```javascript
// File: src/oauthCallback.js
export const handleOAuthCallback = async () => {
  const urlParams = new
URLSearchParams(window.location.search);
  const code = urlParams.get('code');
  if (!code) {
    throw new Error('No authorization code provided');
  }

  const response = await
fetch('https://oauth.example.com/token', {
    method: 'POST',
    headers: { 'Content-Type': 'application/json' },
    body: JSON.stringify({
      client_id: 'YOUR_CLIENT_ID',
      client_secret: 'YOUR_CLIENT_SECRET',
      code,
      grant_type: 'authorization_code',
      redirect_uri: window.location.origin +
'/auth/callback',
    }),
  });

  if (!response.ok) {
    throw new Error('Token exchange failed');
  }

  const { access_token, refresh_token } = await
response.json();
  localStorage.setItem('authToken', access_token);
  localStorage.setItem('refreshToken', refresh_token);
};
```

Personal Insight:
Implementing OAuth can be challenging due to its multi-step nature, but it significantly enhances security and user convenience by leveraging trusted providers.

Session Strategies

Overview

Session-based authentication is a traditional approach where session data is stored on the server, and the client holds a session ID (often in an HTTP-only cookie). This approach centralizes session management on the server.

Practical Client-Side Example

For session-based authentication, you usually rely on the browser to manage cookies automatically. Your API calls must include credentials.

```js
// File: src/auth/loginSession.js
export const loginWithSession = async ({ username, password
}) => {
  const response = await
fetch('https://api.example.com/auth/login', {
    method: 'POST',
    headers: { 'Content-Type': 'application/json' },
    credentials: 'include',  // Ensures cookies are sent
and received
    body: JSON.stringify({ username, password }),
  });

  if (!response.ok) {
    throw new Error('Login failed');
  }

  // Session is maintained via HTTP-only cookies; no token
is stored in JS
  return response.json();
};
```

Personal Insight:
While session strategies are secure—since HTTP-only cookies protect against XSS—they can be trickier in distributed systems or when scaling horizontally. They require careful backend management but provide an extra layer of security by keeping tokens out of JavaScript.

10.3: Implementing Role-Based Access Control (RBAC)

Role-Based Access Control (RBAC) is a critical security strategy for admin dashboards, ensuring that users can only access resources and perform actions appropriate to their role. In this guide, we'll dive into what RBAC is, why it's important, and how to implement it in your React Admin application. We'll walk through practical, step-by-step examples to show you how to enforce access restrictions based on user roles.

Personal Insight:
When I first implemented RBAC in one of my projects, it not only helped secure the application but also made it easier to manage user permissions as the team grew. It allowed for clear separation of privileges, ensuring that only authorized users could access sensitive areas.

What Is RBAC?

RBAC is a method of regulating access where users are assigned roles, and each role has defined permissions. Instead of checking permissions for every user individually, you define roles such as **admin**, **editor**, and **viewer**. Your application then uses these roles to control access to routes, components, and actions.

Key Concepts:

- **Roles:** Labels such as "admin," "editor," or "viewer" that define a set of permissions.
- **Permissions:** Specific rights or actions (e.g., edit posts, delete users) granted to a role.
- **Access Control:** Enforcing restrictions so that only users with the appropriate role can access certain features.

Implementing RBAC in React Admin

There are multiple ways to implement RBAC in a React Admin application. We'll cover two common approaches:

1. **Custom Protected Routes:** Create components that check the user's roles before rendering content.
2. **Conditional Rendering in Components:** Use the getPermissions method from your auth provider to conditionally render UI elements.

Approach 1: Custom Protected Routes

Step 1: Create a Protected Route Component

We can create a reusable ProtectedRoute component that uses React Router to guard routes based on user roles.

```js
// File: src/components/ProtectedRoute.js
import React from 'react';
import { Route, Redirect } from 'react-router-dom';
import { useSelector } from 'react-redux';

const ProtectedRoute = ({ component: Component,
requiredRole, ...rest }) => {
  // Assuming the user's roles are stored in Redux state
under auth.user.roles
  const userRoles = useSelector((state) =>
state.auth.user?.roles || []);

  // Check if the user has the required role
  const isAuthorized = userRoles.includes(requiredRole);

  return (
    <Route
      {...rest}
      render={(props) =>
        isAuthorized ? (
          <Component {...props} />
        ) : (
          <Redirect to="/unauthorized" />
        )
      }
    />
  );
};
```

```
export default ProtectedRoute;
```

Explanation:

- **useSelector Hook:** Retrieves the current user's roles from the Redux store.
- **Role Check:** Verifies if the `requiredRole` is included in the user's roles.
- **Conditional Rendering:** Renders the protected component if authorized; otherwise, it redirects to an unauthorized page.

Step 2: Use the Protected Route Component

Integrate the `ProtectedRoute` into your routing setup:

```
// File: src/App.js
import React from 'react';
import { BrowserRouter as Router, Switch, Route } from
'react-router-dom';
import ProtectedRoute from './components/ProtectedRoute';
import Dashboard from './pages/Dashboard';
import AdminPage from './pages/AdminPage';
import Unauthorized from './pages/Unauthorized';

const App = () => (
  <Router>
    <Switch>
      <Route exact path="/" component={Dashboard} />
      <ProtectedRoute path="/admin" component={AdminPage}
requiredRole="admin" />
      <Route path="/unauthorized" component={Unauthorized}
/>
    </Switch>
  </Router>
);

export default App;
```

Explanation:

- **Routing Setup:** Uses `ProtectedRoute` for the `/admin` route, ensuring that only users with the "admin" role can access it.
- **Unauthorized Page:** Redirects users without proper permissions to a dedicated unauthorized page.

Personal Insight:
Creating protected routes early in your project enforces a clean separation of concerns. It's much easier to manage permissions at the route level than to scatter role checks throughout your components.

Approach 2: Conditional Rendering in Components

Instead of protecting routes, you can also hide or show specific UI elements based on user roles. This is useful for displaying different menu options or buttons.

Step 1: Using getPermissions from the Auth Provider

React Admin's auth provider often includes a `getPermissions` method. You can use this method with the `usePermissions` hook to control what gets rendered.

```
// File: src/components/CustomMenu.js
import React from 'react';
import { usePermissions, MenuItemLink } from 'react-admin';

const CustomMenu = (props) => {
  const { permissions } = usePermissions();

  return (
    <div>
      <MenuItemLink to="/dashboard" primaryText="Dashboard"
{...props} />
      {permissions.includes('admin') && (
        <MenuItemLink to="/admin" primaryText="Admin Panel"
{...props} />
      )}
      {permissions.includes('editor') && (
        <MenuItemLink to="/editor" primaryText="Editor
Tools" {...props} />
      )}
    </div>
  );
};

export default CustomMenu;
```

Explanation:

- **usePermissions Hook:** Retrieves the current user's permissions.
- **Conditional Rendering:** Menu items are rendered based on the user's roles, ensuring only authorized options are visible.

Personal Insight:
I've used conditional rendering in menus and toolbars to tailor the user experience. It makes the interface less cluttered and ensures that users are only presented with actions they're allowed to perform.

Best Practices for Implementing RBAC

1. **Centralize Role Data:**
   Store user roles in a global state (e.g., Redux) or use React Admin's auth provider. This makes it easier to manage and access roles throughout the application.
2. **Consistent Naming:**
   Use consistent role names (e.g., "admin," "editor," "viewer") across your application to avoid confusion.
3. **Graceful Fallbacks:**
   Always provide fallback UI (such as an unauthorized page or a message) when users try to access restricted areas.
4. **Regularly Review Permissions:**
   As your application evolves, revisit and update roles and permissions to ensure they still align with your security requirements.

Personal Insight:
Implementing RBAC transformed my approach to application security. It was challenging at first to determine the right granularity for roles, but once established, it greatly simplified both the development and maintenance processes. The clear boundaries also improved collaboration with non-technical stakeholders who could easily understand access levels.

10.4: Securing API Endpoints and Sensitive Data

Securing your API endpoints and protecting sensitive data is critical in any production application, especially in admin dashboards where confidential information is frequently handled. In this guide, we'll dive into the strategies and best practices for securing your backend services. We'll discuss topics such as authentication, authorization, HTTPS, rate limiting, input validation, and data encryption. Along the way, I'll provide step-by-step, practical code examples and share personal insights to help you implement these strategies effectively.

Personal Insight:
Early in my career, I underestimated the importance of API security. After experiencing a few security incidents, I realized that a robust, multi-layered security approach not only protects sensitive data but also builds user trust. Let's explore how to fortify your API endpoints.

---

1. Authentication and Authorization

A. Token-Based Authentication

Most modern APIs use token-based authentication, such as JWT, to verify the identity of a user. On the server side, you need middleware to check that incoming requests include a valid token.

Step-by-Step Example: Securing an Endpoint with JWT

1. **Install Dependencies:**

```
npm install express jsonwebtoken dotenv
```

2. **Set Up Environment Variables:**

   Create a `.env` file with a secret key:

```
JWT_SECRET=your_super_secret_key
```

3. Create Authentication Middleware:

```javascript
// File: server/authMiddleware.js
const jwt = require('jsonwebtoken');
require('dotenv').config();

const authenticateToken = (req, res, next) => {
  const authHeader = req.headers['authorization'];
  const token = authHeader && authHeader.split(' ')[1];
  if (!token) return res.sendStatus(401); // Unauthorized

  jwt.verify(token, process.env.JWT_SECRET, (err, user) =>
{
    if (err) return res.sendStatus(403); // Forbidden
    req.user = user;
    next();
  });
};

module.exports = authenticateToken;
```

4. Secure an API Endpoint:

```javascript
// File: server/server.js
const express = require('express');
const jwt = require('jsonwebtoken');
const authenticateToken = require('./authMiddleware');
require('dotenv').config();

const app = express();
app.use(express.json());

// Public route for login (for demonstration purposes)
app.post('/login', (req, res) => {
  // In a real app, you'd verify user credentials here.
  const username = req.body.username;
  const user = { name: username, roles: ['admin'] };

  // Sign a JWT token
  const token = jwt.sign(user, process.env.JWT_SECRET, {
expiresIn: '1h' });
  res.json({ token });
});

// Protected endpoint
app.get('/api/sensitive-data', authenticateToken, (req,
res) => {
  // Further role-based checks can be done here if needed
  if (!req.user.roles.includes('admin')) {
```

```
    return res.sendStatus(403); // Forbidden
  }
  res.json({ data: 'Sensitive data that only authorized
users can see.' });
});

app.listen(3000, () => {
  console.log('Server running on port 3000');
});
```

Explanation:

- **Authentication Middleware:** Validates the JWT from the Authorization header.
- **Endpoint Security:** The `/api/sensitive-data` route is protected, only allowing access if a valid token is provided and the user has the necessary role.
- **JWT Management:** The login route signs a JWT token which includes user roles for further authorization.

2. HTTPS and Secure Communication

Why HTTPS Matters

Using HTTPS encrypts data transmitted between the client and server, preventing eavesdropping and man-in-the-middle attacks.

- **Implementation:**
  Configure your server (or use a reverse proxy like Nginx) with an SSL certificate.
- **Best Practice:**
  Always enforce HTTPS in production, and consider HTTP Strict Transport Security (HSTS) to ensure browsers always connect securely.

Personal Insight:
Moving to HTTPS was a significant step in securing my applications. It not only boosted security but also improved user trust and even SEO rankings.

3. Rate Limiting and Throttling

Purpose

Rate limiting controls the number of requests a client can make in a given time frame, protecting your API from abuse and denial-of-service (DoS) attacks.

Implementation Example with Express Middleware

1. Install the Rate Limiter:

```
npm install express-rate-limit
```

2. Configure Rate Limiting:

```javascript
// File: server/rateLimiter.js
const rateLimit = require('express-rate-limit');

const limiter = rateLimit({
  windowMs: 15 * 60 * 1000, // 15 minutes
  max: 100, // Limit each IP to 100 requests per windowMs
  message: 'Too many requests from this IP, please try
again later.',
});

module.exports = limiter;
```

3. Apply Rate Limiting to Your Server:

```javascript
// File: server/server.js (update)
const limiter = require('./rateLimiter');

// Apply to all requests
app.use(limiter);
```

Personal Insight:
Implementing rate limiting was crucial during load testing; it helped prevent accidental DoS-like scenarios and kept our server performance in check.

4. Input Validation and Sanitization

Why Validate Input

Validating and sanitizing inputs prevents common vulnerabilities such as SQL injection, XSS, and other malicious exploits.

Implementation Example with Express Validator

1. **Install Express Validator:**

```
npm install express-validator
```

2. **Apply Validation in Routes:**

```javascript
// File: server/routes.js
const express = require('express');
const { body, validationResult } = require('express-validator');
const router = express.Router();

router.post(
  '/api/posts',
  [
    body('title').isString().notEmpty(),
    body('content').isString().notEmpty(),
  ],
  (req, res) => {
    const errors = validationResult(req);
    if (!errors.isEmpty()) {
      return res.status(400).json({ errors: errors.array() });
    }
    // Proceed with creating the post
    res.json({ message: 'Post created successfully' });
  }
);

module.exports = router;
```

Personal Insight:
I once faced a security audit that highlighted the need for robust input validation. Integrating libraries like express-validator not only improved security but also made the codebase cleaner and easier to maintain.

5. Encrypting Sensitive Data

At Rest and In Transit

- **In Transit:**
  Use HTTPS to encrypt data during transmission.
- **At Rest:**
  Encrypt sensitive data stored in databases. Tools and libraries such as bcrypt for passwords or database-specific encryption methods should be used.

Example: Hashing Passwords with bcrypt

1. **Install bcrypt:**

```
npm install bcrypt
```

2. **Hashing a Password:**

```javascript
// File: server/hashPassword.js
const bcrypt = require('bcrypt');

const hashPassword = async (plainTextPassword) => {
  const saltRounds = 10;
  return await bcrypt.hash(plainTextPassword, saltRounds);
};

// Usage example:
hashPassword('mySecurePassword')
  .then(hash => console.log('Hashed password:', hash))
  .catch(err => console.error(err));
```

Personal Insight:
Encrypting data, particularly user passwords, is non-negotiable. Using bcrypt not only secures the data but also significantly reduces the risk of data breaches that could compromise sensitive information.

Securing API endpoints and sensitive data requires a multi-layered approach. By combining token-based authentication (with JWTs, OAuth, or sessions), enforcing HTTPS, applying rate limiting, validating inputs, and encrypting sensitive data, you create a robust defense against common security threats.

Chapter 11: Data Visualization and Reporting

In today's data-driven world, transforming raw data into clear, actionable insights is key to empowering decision-makers. In this chapter, we'll explore how to create compelling visualizations and comprehensive reports in your React Admin dashboard. We'll cover selecting the right chart library, building interactive and responsive data visualizations, best practices for accessible and usable reporting, and integrating dashboards with real-time metrics.

Personal Insight:
Throughout my career, I've seen how well-designed data visualizations can turn complex datasets into intuitive stories. Whether it's a line chart showing sales trends or an interactive dashboard for monitoring system performance, effective visualizations help users quickly grasp key insights and make informed decisions.

11.1: Selecting the Right Chart Library (Chart.js, Recharts, D3.js)

Choosing the right chart library is a critical decision when designing data visualizations for your admin dashboard. The ideal library should not only meet your project's requirements in terms of functionality and customization but also integrate seamlessly with your React application. In this guide, we'll explore three popular libraries—Chart.js, Recharts, and D3.js—analyze their strengths and weaknesses, and provide practical, step-by-step examples to help you decide which one fits your needs.

Personal Insight:
I've experimented with multiple charting libraries over the years, and each has its own niche. For instance, Chart.js is fantastic for quick, standard charts, while D3.js offers unmatched flexibility for custom visualizations. Recharts, on the other hand, strikes a balance by being built specifically for React. Let's dive in!

1. Chart.js

Overview

Chart.js is a simple yet powerful library that supports a variety of chart types such as line, bar, pie, radar, and more. It is known for its ease of use, appealing default designs, and responsiveness.

Pros

- **User-Friendly API:**
  Easy to set up and customize for standard chart types.
- **Responsive:**
  Out of the box, it produces responsive charts.
- **Lightweight:**
  Minimal overhead makes it ideal for simple projects.

Cons

- **Limited Customization:**
  For highly interactive or custom visualizations, you may find Chart.js less flexible.
- **Integration with React:**
  Although there are React wrappers available (like `react-chartjs-2`), integration is not as native as with React-specific libraries.

Practical Example: Creating a Simple Bar Chart with Chart.js

1. **Install `react-chartjs-2` and `chart.js`:**

```
npm install react-chartjs-2 chart.js
```

2. **Create the Bar Chart Component:**

```
// File: src/components/ChartJsBarChart.js
import React from 'react';
import { Bar } from 'react-chartjs-2';
```

```
import { Chart as ChartJS, CategoryScale, LinearScale,
BarElement, Title, Tooltip, Legend } from 'chart.js';

ChartJS.register(CategoryScale, LinearScale, BarElement,
Title, Tooltip, Legend);

const data = {
  labels: ['January', 'February', 'March', 'April', 'May'],
  datasets: [
    {
      label: 'Sales',
      data: [300, 500, 400, 700, 600],
      backgroundColor: 'rgba(75,192,192,0.6)',
    },
  ],
};

const options = {
  responsive: true,
  plugins: {
    legend: { position: 'top' },
    title: { display: true, text: 'Monthly Sales' },
  },
};

const ChartJsBarChart = () => (
  <div>
    <Bar data={data} options={options} />
  </div>
);

export default ChartJsBarChart;
```

3. **Usage in Your App:**

```
// File: src/App.js
import React from 'react';
import ChartJsBarChart from './components/ChartJsBarChart';

const App = () => (
  <div style={{ width: '600px', margin: '0 auto' }}>
    <h1>Chart.js Example</h1>
    <ChartJsBarChart />
  </div>
);

export default App;
```

Personal Insight:
Chart.js is my go-to when I need a quick, attractive chart with minimal fuss. Its simplicity allows me to focus on the data rather than the underlying implementation.

---

2. Recharts

Overview

Recharts is built specifically for React, offering a collection of composable chart components that make it simple to create responsive and customizable visualizations. It uses D3.js under the hood for calculations but abstracts away much of the complexity.

Pros

- **React-Friendly:**
  Designed with React in mind, which means easier integration and better state management.
- **Customizable Components:**
  Provides a wide range of chart types and allows for detailed customization.
- **Responsive by Default:**
  Uses container components that automatically adjust to different screen sizes.

Cons

- **Limited for Complex Visualizations:**
  While excellent for standard charts, highly customized or interactive visualizations may require more flexibility than Recharts offers.
- **Performance with Large Datasets:**
  May not be as efficient as lower-level libraries like D3.js for very large data sets.

Practical Example: Creating a Responsive Bar Chart with Recharts

1. **Install Recharts:**

```
npm install recharts
```

2. **Create the Bar Chart Component:**

```js
// File: src/components/RechartsBarChart.js
import React from 'react';
import { ResponsiveContainer, BarChart, Bar, XAxis, YAxis,
CartesianGrid, Tooltip, Legend } from 'recharts';

const data = [
  { month: 'January', sales: 300 },
  { month: 'February', sales: 500 },
  { month: 'March', sales: 400 },
  { month: 'April', sales: 700 },
  { month: 'May', sales: 600 },
];

const RechartsBarChart = () => (
  <ResponsiveContainer width="100%" height={300}>
    <BarChart data={data} margin={{ top: 20, right: 30,
left: 20, bottom: 5 }}>
      <CartesianGrid strokeDasharray="3 3" />
      <XAxis dataKey="month" />
      <YAxis />
      <Tooltip />
      <Legend />
      <Bar dataKey="sales" fill="#8884d8" />
    </BarChart>
  </ResponsiveContainer>
);

export default RechartsBarChart;
```

3. **Usage in Your App:**

```js
// File: src/App.js
import React from 'react';
import RechartsBarChart from
'./components/RechartsBarChart';

const App = () => (
  <div style={{ width: '80%', margin: '0 auto' }}>
    <h1>Recharts Example</h1>
    <RechartsBarChart />
  </div>
);
```

```
export default App;
```

Personal Insight:
Recharts feels very natural in a React ecosystem. Its components are intuitive, and the integration with React state and props makes it easy to create dynamic, responsive charts. I appreciate its balance between simplicity and customization.

---

3. D3.js

Overview

D3.js is a powerful and flexible data visualization library that provides granular control over your visualizations. It excels at creating custom, highly interactive, and complex visualizations that are tailored to your specific data needs.

Pros

- **Extremely Flexible:**
  Allows you to create virtually any type of visualization.
- **Fine-Grained Control:**
  Direct manipulation of the DOM for detailed customizations.
- **Wide Community and Resources:**
  A vast array of examples and plugins are available.

Cons

- **Steep Learning Curve:**
  Requires a deeper understanding of data manipulation and the DOM.
- **Integration Complexity:**
  Integrating D3.js directly into React can be challenging due to differences in how both libraries manage the DOM.
- **More Boilerplate Code:**
  You often have to write more code compared to higher-level libraries.

Practical Example: A Simple Bar Chart with D3.js in React

Integrating D3 with React typically involves using D3 for calculations and then letting React handle rendering, or using D3 to manipulate an SVG element created by React.

1. **Install D3.js:**

```
npm install d3
```

2. **Create the D3 Bar Chart Component:**

```javascript
// File: src/components/D3BarChart.js
import React, { useEffect, useRef } from 'react';
import * as d3 from 'd3';

const data = [
  { month: 'January', sales: 300 },
  { month: 'February', sales: 500 },
  { month: 'March', sales: 400 },
  { month: 'April', sales: 700 },
  { month: 'May', sales: 600 },
];

const D3BarChart = () => {
  const svgRef = useRef();

  useEffect(() => {
    const svg = d3.select(svgRef.current);
    const width = 600;
    const height = 300;
    const margin = { top: 20, right: 30, bottom: 30, left: 40 };

    // Clear previous rendering
    svg.selectAll('*').remove();

    // Set up scales
    const x = d3.scaleBand()
      .domain(data.map(d => d.month))
      .range([margin.left, width - margin.right])
      .padding(0.1);

    const y = d3.scaleLinear()
      .domain([0, d3.max(data, d => d.sales)])
      .nice()
      .range([height - margin.bottom, margin.top]);

    // Draw X-axis
    svg.append('g')
```

```
      .attr('transform', `translate(0,${height -
margin.bottom})`)
      .call(d3.axisBottom(x));

    // Draw Y-axis
    svg.append('g')
      .attr('transform', `translate(${margin.left},0)`)
      .call(d3.axisLeft(y));

    // Draw bars
    svg.append('g')
      .selectAll('rect')
      .data(data)
      .enter()
      .append('rect')
      .attr('x', d => x(d.month))
      .attr('y', d => y(d.sales))
      .attr('height', d => y(0) - y(d.sales))
      .attr('width', x.bandwidth())
      .attr('fill', '#69b3a2');
  }, []);

  return (
    <div>
      <h3>D3.js Bar Chart</h3>
      <svg ref={svgRef} width={600} height={300}></svg>
    </div>
  );
};

export default D3BarChart;
```

3. Usage in Your App:

```
// File: src/App.js
import React from 'react';
import D3BarChart from './components/D3BarChart';

const App = () => (
  <div style={{ display: 'flex', justifyContent: 'center',
marginTop: '2rem' }}>
    <D3BarChart />
  </div>
);

export default App;
```

Personal Insight:
D3.js gives you unparalleled control over your data visualizations. While

it requires a bit more work compared to Chart.js or Recharts, the level of customization and interactivity you can achieve is impressive. I often turn to D3 when I need to create a unique or highly specialized visualization that goes beyond standard chart types.

11.2: Creating Interactive and Responsive Data Visualizations

Data visualizations become truly powerful when they allow users to explore and interact with data in real time. In this section, we'll discuss how to build visualizations that are both interactive and responsive— ensuring they adapt to different devices and encourage user engagement. We'll use a step-by-step approach with practical code examples and insights to guide you through the process.

Personal Insight:
I've seen firsthand how interactivity transforms static charts into dynamic tools that empower users. Adding features like tooltips, clickable legends, and real-time updates can make complex data much easier to understand. Let's dive in!

Why Interactivity and Responsiveness Matter

- **Interactivity:**
  Interactive visualizations allow users to drill down into data, hover for more details, and even filter or update charts on the fly. This engagement helps users uncover insights that might be missed in static graphs.
- **Responsiveness:**
  Responsive visualizations adjust seamlessly to various screen sizes and orientations. This ensures that your dashboard remains usable on devices ranging from mobile phones to large desktop monitors.

Tools and Techniques

For our examples, we'll use **Recharts**—a React-specific charting library that makes it easy to create responsive and interactive visualizations. Recharts integrates naturally with React and provides components such as `ResponsiveContainer`, `LineChart`, `BarChart`, and more.

Step-by-Step Example: Building an Interactive and Responsive Line Chart

Step 1: Install Recharts

First, ensure that Recharts is installed in your project:

```
npm install recharts
```

Step 2: Create the Interactive Line Chart Component

Below is a complete example of an interactive line chart. In this chart, users can hover over data points to see detailed tooltips, and we include a button to simulate a data update.

```js
// File: src/components/InteractiveLineChart.js
import React, { useState } from 'react';
import {
  ResponsiveContainer,
  LineChart,
  Line,
  XAxis,
  YAxis,
  CartesianGrid,
  Tooltip,
  Legend,
} from 'recharts';

const initialData = [
  { time: '08:00', value: 50 },
  { time: '09:00', value: 75 },
  { time: '10:00', value: 100 },
  { time: '11:00', value: 125 },
  { time: '12:00', value: 150 },
];

const InteractiveLineChart = () => {
```

```
  const [data, setData] = useState(initialData);

  // Simulate data update for interactivity
  const updateData = () => {
    setData((prevData) =>
      prevData.map((d) => ({ ...d, value: d.value +
Math.floor(Math.random() * 20) }))
    );
  };

  return (
    <div style={{ textAlign: 'center', marginTop: '2rem'
}}>
      <h2>Interactive Line Chart</h2>
      <button onClick={updateData} style={{ marginBottom:
'1rem', padding: '0.5rem 1rem' }}>
        Update Data
      </button>
      <ResponsiveContainer width="100%" height={300}>
        <LineChart
          data={data}
          margin={{ top: 20, right: 30, left: 20, bottom: 5
}}
          onClick={(e) => {
            if (e && e.activePayload) {
              console.log('Data point clicked:',
e.activePayload[0].payload);
            }
          }}
        >
          <CartesianGrid strokeDasharray="3 3" />
          <XAxis dataKey="time" />
          <YAxis />
          <Tooltip />
          <Legend />
          <Line type="monotone" dataKey="value"
stroke="#82ca9d" activeDot={{ r: 8 }} />
        </LineChart>
      </ResponsiveContainer>
    </div>
  );
};

export default InteractiveLineChart;
```

Explanation:

- **ResponsiveContainer:**
  Wraps the chart to ensure it adjusts to the width and height of its parent container.
- **LineChart and Axes:**
  The `LineChart` is configured with margins, and `XAxis` and `YAxis` display the time and value respectively.
- **Tooltip and Legend:**
  These components provide interactivity, showing data details on hover and a legend for clarity.
- **Data Update Button:**
  The `updateData` function simulates changes by updating the data points with random increments, demonstrating how interactivity can reflect dynamic data.
- **onClick Handler:**
  Clicking on the chart logs the clicked data point, showcasing how you can add custom interactivity to your visualizations.

Personal Insight:
I love how Recharts makes it simple to add interactivity with minimal code. The ability to update data dynamically and handle user events (like clicks) gives you the power to build truly engaging dashboards.

Best Practices for Interactive and Responsive Visualizations

1. **Keep It Simple:**
   Avoid clutter by focusing on key metrics. Use interactive elements like tooltips and legends to provide additional details without overwhelming the user.
2. **Optimize for Touch:**
   Ensure that interactive elements are accessible on touch devices. Use larger touch targets and consider gesture support.
3. **Test Responsiveness:**
   Regularly test your visualizations on multiple devices to ensure they scale well. Use tools like Chrome DevTools for responsive design testing.
4. **Performance Considerations:**
   For complex charts, optimize data processing to prevent slow

rendering. Techniques like memoization can help maintain performance.
5. **Accessibility:**
   Incorporate ARIA labels and ensure your charts are navigable via keyboard and screen readers.

Personal Insight:
A well-designed interactive visualization not only presents data but tells a story. I've found that investing time in refining interactivity and responsiveness pays off by making the dashboard more engaging and insightful for end users.

Creating interactive and responsive data visualizations is a vital part of building effective admin dashboards. By leveraging tools like Recharts, you can craft charts that adapt to various devices and invite users to explore data in real time. The example provided demonstrates a practical approach to building an interactive line chart, complete with dynamic data updates and user event handling.

11.3: Best Practices for Accessible and Usable Reporting

Creating data reports and visualizations isn't just about displaying numbers and charts—it's about communicating insights clearly and ensuring that everyone, regardless of ability, can access and understand the data. In this guide, we'll dive into best practices for building accessible and usable reporting interfaces. We'll cover guidelines for ensuring that reports are inclusive, provide actionable insights, and are easy to navigate. Along the way, we'll provide practical, step-by-step examples and share personal insights to help you implement these practices effectively.

Personal Insight:
I've found that making reports accessible not only broadens the reach of your application but also forces you to design clearer and more user-friendly interfaces. When reports are easy to navigate and understand, users can make decisions faster, which is a win-win for everyone.

1. Why Accessible and Usable Reporting Matters

Accessibility

Accessible reporting ensures that all users—including those with visual, auditory, or motor impairments—can access, interact with, and benefit from your data. This involves:

- **Screen Reader Compatibility:** Use proper semantic markup and ARIA attributes.
- **Keyboard Navigation:** Ensure that users who cannot use a mouse can still navigate through charts and tables.
- **Color Contrast:** Provide sufficient contrast so that information is readable for users with low vision.

Usability

Usable reporting focuses on delivering information in a clear, concise, and actionable way:

- **Clear Visual Hierarchy:** Use headings, labels, and legends to organize data.
- **Interactive Elements:** Enable users to filter, sort, or drill down into data.
- **Responsive Design:** Ensure that reports adapt gracefully to various screen sizes, from mobile to desktop.

---

2. Best Practices for Accessible Reporting

A. Use Semantic HTML and ARIA Attributes

When building reports, use semantic HTML elements where possible. For instance, use `<table>` elements for tabular data and `<figure>` with `<figcaption>` for charts. Enhance these with ARIA roles and attributes.

Example: Accessible Data Table

```javascript
// File: src/components/AccessibleDataTable.js
import React from 'react';

const AccessibleDataTable = ({ data }) => (
  <table aria-label="Sales Data Table" style={{ width:
'100%', borderCollapse: 'collapse' }}>
    <caption style={{ textAlign: 'left', fontWeight:
'bold', marginBottom: '0.5rem' }}>
      Monthly Sales Data
    </caption>
    <thead>
      <tr>
        <th scope="col" style={{ borderBottom: '2px solid
#333', padding: '0.5rem' }}>Month</th>
        <th scope="col" style={{ borderBottom: '2px solid
#333', padding: '0.5rem' }}>Sales</th>
      </tr>
    </thead>
    <tbody>
      {data.map((row, index) => (
        <tr key={index}>
          <td style={{ borderBottom: '1px solid #ccc',
padding: '0.5rem' }}>{row.month}</td>
          <td style={{ borderBottom: '1px solid #ccc',
padding: '0.5rem' }}>{row.sales}</td>
        </tr>
      ))}
    </tbody>
  </table>
);

export default AccessibleDataTable;
```

Explanation:

- The `<caption>` element provides context for the table.
- `scope` attributes on `<th>` elements help screen readers understand table structure.
- Inline styles ensure a clean, readable table.

B. Ensure Keyboard Navigability

All interactive elements, such as charts with tooltips or data filters, should be accessible via keyboard. Use focusable elements (e.g., `<button>`, `<a>`) and manage focus order logically.

Example: Keyboard-Navigable Chart Controls

```
// File: src/components/ChartControls.js
import React from 'react';

const ChartControls = ({ onFilterChange }) => (
  <div>
    <label htmlFor="filter">Filter Data:</label>
    <input
      id="filter"
      type="text"
      onChange={(e) => onFilterChange(e.target.value)}
      style={{ padding: '0.5rem', margin: '0.5rem 0' }}
    />
    <button onClick={() => onFilterChange('')} style={{
padding: '0.5rem 1rem' }}>
      Clear Filter
    </button>
  </div>
);

export default ChartControls;
```

Explanation:

- Labels and inputs are linked using `htmlFor` and `id`.
- Buttons are accessible via keyboard by default.

C. Maintain Sufficient Color Contrast and Use Accessible Colors

Ensure that your color scheme meets WCAG guidelines for contrast. This helps users with low vision or color blindness.

Example: Accessible Chart Colors with Recharts

```
// File: src/components/AccessibleChart.js
import React from 'react';
import { ResponsiveContainer, LineChart, Line, XAxis,
YAxis, Tooltip, Legend } from 'recharts';

const data = [
  { time: '08:00', value: 50 },
  { time: '09:00', value: 75 },
  { time: '10:00', value: 100 },
  { time: '11:00', value: 125 },
  { time: '12:00', value: 150 },
];
```

```
const AccessibleChart = () => (
  <ResponsiveContainer width="100%" height={300}>
    <LineChart data={data}>
      <XAxis dataKey="time" aria-label="Time of day" />
      <YAxis aria-label="Value" />
      <Tooltip />
      <Legend />
      <Line
        type="monotone"
        dataKey="value"
        stroke="#005f73" // High-contrast color
        strokeWidth={2}
        activeDot={{ r: 8 }}
        aria-label="Sales over time"
      />
    </LineChart>
  </ResponsiveContainer>
);

export default AccessibleChart;
```

Explanation:

- Choose colors with high contrast, like dark teal on a light background.
- ARIA labels are used to provide context for screen readers.

D. Provide Clear Documentation and Tooltips

Interactive charts should include tooltips that explain data points, and charts should have clear legends and labels. This ensures users understand what they're viewing.

Personal Insight:
One of the biggest lessons I learned was that clarity is king. Users are more likely to trust and use a dashboard that explains its data clearly. Always consider adding descriptive tooltips and legends, as they can significantly improve user experience.

---

3. Usability Best Practices for Reporting

A. Clear Visual Hierarchy

Organize your reports with headings, subheadings, and consistent styling. This helps users quickly understand the structure and flow of information.

B. Responsive Design

Ensure that your reports adjust gracefully to different screen sizes. Use responsive containers and media queries to tailor the layout for mobile, tablet, and desktop views.

C. Interactivity Without Overwhelm

Provide interactive elements like filters, drill-downs, and dynamic updates, but avoid clutter. Aim for simplicity—display only essential data, and allow users to explore further if needed.

D. Consistent Layout and Navigation

Keep navigation elements consistent across reports. This includes menus, breadcrumbs, and action buttons. Consistency makes your dashboard easier to learn and use.

Accessible and usable reporting is about creating data visualizations that everyone can interact with, understand, and benefit from. By following best practices—such as using semantic HTML, ensuring keyboard navigability, maintaining sufficient color contrast, and providing clear documentation—you can build dashboards that are both inclusive and effective.

11.4: Integrating Dashboards with Real-Time Metrics

Integrating real-time metrics into your dashboards can elevate your admin interface from static reporting to a dynamic, live data experience. Real-time data empowers users to monitor critical metrics as they happen—whether it's tracking website traffic, monitoring system performance, or viewing sales trends. In this guide, we'll explore the benefits of real-time dashboards, discuss key integration strategies, and walk through a complete, step-by-step example using WebSockets to update a dashboard in real time.

Personal Insight:
I remember the excitement of watching live data flow into a dashboard during a critical product launch. Real-time metrics not only improve decision-making but also boost user engagement by providing immediate, actionable insights.

Overview: Why Real-Time Metrics Matter

Real-time dashboards allow users to:

- **Monitor Performance:** Instantly identify trends, spikes, or drops in key metrics.
- **Make Informed Decisions:** React quickly to new data, improving overall responsiveness.
- **Enhance User Engagement:** Provide a dynamic interface that feels modern and proactive.

Key Integration Strategies

1. **WebSockets:**
   Establish a persistent connection between client and server for bi-directional data flow. Ideal for scenarios where the server sends updates frequently.
2. **Server-Sent Events (SSE):**
   Use SSE for a simpler, unidirectional data stream from server to client. SSE is easier to set up for cases where only the server needs to push updates.
3. **Polling:**
   Periodically fetch data from the server. This is the simplest method but may not be as efficient as WebSockets or SSE for high-frequency updates.

For this guide, we'll focus on integrating real-time metrics using WebSockets, as they provide a robust solution for live, interactive dashboards.

Step-by-Step Example: Real-Time Dashboard with WebSockets

Step 1: Create a WebSocket Client

We start by building a simple WebSocket client that handles the connection, listens for messages, and closes the connection when needed.

```js
// File: src/websocketClient.js
class WebSocketClient {
  constructor(url) {
    this.socket = new WebSocket(url);
  }

  // Register a callback for incoming messages
  onMessage(callback) {
    this.socket.onmessage = (event) => {
      const data = JSON.parse(event.data);
      callback(data);
    };
  }

  // Send data to the server (if needed)
  send(data) {
    this.socket.send(JSON.stringify(data));
  }

  // Close the WebSocket connection
  close() {
    this.socket.close();
  }
}

export default WebSocketClient;
```

Explanation:
This client wraps the native WebSocket API to simplify message handling in our React components.

Step 2: Build the Real-Time Dashboard Component

Next, we'll build a dashboard component that listens for real-time updates from our WebSocket server and updates the UI accordingly.

```
// File: src/components/RealTimeDashboard.js
import React, { useEffect, useState } from 'react';
import { ResponsiveContainer, LineChart, Line, XAxis,
YAxis, Tooltip, CartesianGrid } from 'recharts';
import WebSocketClient from '../websocketClient';

const RealTimeDashboard = () => {
  const [metrics, setMetrics] = useState([]);

  useEffect(() => {
    // Replace with your actual WebSocket server URL
    const client = new WebSocketClient('wss://your-
websocket-server-url');

    // Listen for real-time updates
    client.onMessage((data) => {
      // For simplicity, assume data contains a timestamp
and a metric value
      setMetrics((prevMetrics) => {
        // Limit to the latest 20 data points for clarity
        const updatedMetrics = [data, ...prevMetrics];
        return updatedMetrics.slice(0, 20);
      });
    });

    // Clean up on component unmount
    return () => client.close();
  }, []);

  return (
    <div style={{ margin: '2rem auto', width: '90%' }}>
      <h2 style={{ textAlign: 'center' }}>Real-Time Metrics
Dashboard</h2>
      <ResponsiveContainer width="100%" height={300}>
        <LineChart data={metrics} margin={{ top: 20, right:
30, left: 20, bottom: 5 }}>
          <CartesianGrid strokeDasharray="3 3" />
          <XAxis dataKey="timestamp" tickFormatter={(ts) =>
new Date(ts).toLocaleTimeString()} />
          <YAxis />
          <Tooltip labelFormatter={(ts) => new
Date(ts).toLocaleTimeString()} />
          <Line type="monotone" dataKey="value"
stroke="#ff7300" strokeWidth={2} dot={{ r: 3 }} />
        </LineChart>
      </ResponsiveContainer>
    </div>
```

```
    );
};

export default RealTimeDashboard;
```

Explanation:

- **State Management:**
  We maintain a state variable `metrics` to store real-time data points.
- **WebSocket Integration:**
  Using our custom WebSocket client, the component listens for incoming messages and updates the state.
- **Data Limiting:**
  For clarity, we retain only the latest 20 data points.
- **Responsive Visualization:**
  The `ResponsiveContainer` ensures the chart adapts to the container size.
- **Chart Components:**
  The `LineChart` and its child components (like `XAxis`, `YAxis`, and `Tooltip`) create an interactive, dynamic visualization that updates as new data arrives.

Personal Insight:
Seeing live data update in real time on a dashboard is incredibly satisfying. In one project, integrating WebSocket-based updates transformed our static metrics view into an interactive monitoring tool, enabling the team to spot and respond to issues almost instantly.

Step 3: Integrate the Real-Time Dashboard into Your Application

Finally, add the `RealTimeDashboard` component to your main application to complete the integration.

```
// File: src/App.js
import React from 'react';
import RealTimeDashboard from
'./components/RealTimeDashboard';

const App = () => (
```

```
  <div>
    <RealTimeDashboard />
  </div>
);

export default App;
```

Explanation:

- This integration is straightforward—simply render the
  RealTimeDashboard component within your app's layout.

Integrating real-time metrics into your dashboards can dramatically improve the user experience by providing up-to-the-minute insights. In this guide, we explored how to:

- **Set Up a WebSocket Client:**
  Abstract the connection and message handling for real-time data.
- **Build a Real-Time Dashboard Component:**
  Use React state and Recharts to create an interactive, responsive visualization.
- **Integrate into Your App:**
  Seamlessly add real-time updates to your admin interface.

By following these steps and adapting the code examples to your needs, you can create a dynamic dashboard that keeps users informed and engaged with live data. Experiment with different chart types, data sources, and real-time integration methods to find the perfect balance for your application.

Conclusion

In this final chapter, we'll wrap up our journey through Professional React Admin Development. We'll summarize the key concepts and techniques covered throughout the book, explore future trends in React Admin development, and offer recommendations for further learning to help you continue growing as a developer.

C 1: Summarizing Key Concepts and Techniques

Throughout this book, we've explored the many facets of building advanced admin dashboards with React Admin. Here's a brief recap of the core topics we covered:

Environment Setup and Project Structure

- **Tooling:** We started by setting up Node.js, npm, and a modern code editor, ensuring you have a solid foundation for React development.
- **Project Bootstrapping:** Using Create React App, we quickly scaffolded a new project, and we discussed how to organize your files and directories to maintain clarity as your project grows.

React Components and Architecture

- **Functional Components and Hooks:**
  We learned how to use functional components with Hooks like `useState` and `useEffect` to manage local state and side effects, making our components more predictable and easier to maintain.
- **Component Composition:**
  By breaking down our UI into smaller, reusable components, we embraced a modular architecture that simplifies both development and debugging.
- **Styling Approaches:**
  We compared traditional CSS, CSS-in-JS (using styled-

components), and Material-UI, ensuring our admin dashboards are both visually appealing and responsive.

State Management

- **Intermediate State Techniques:**
  From local state management with Hooks to sharing state using the Context API and managing complex state with `useReducer`, we covered strategies for building scalable applications.
- **Global State Management:**
  We dove into Redux and its alternatives, discussing how to integrate Redux with React Admin, manage asynchronous data with middleware like Redux Thunk and Redux Saga, and normalize your state for better performance and maintainability.

Performance Optimization

- **Rendering Cycle and Re-render Prevention:**
  We demystified React's rendering cycle, and learned how to use tools like `React.memo`, `useCallback`, and `useMemo` to prevent unnecessary re-renders.
- **Code Splitting and Lazy Loading:**
  By splitting our code into smaller bundles and loading components on demand, we improved our app's initial load time and overall performance.
- **Virtualization:**
  Techniques such as react-window allow you to handle large data sets efficiently, ensuring a smooth user experience even with thousands of records.

Advanced API Integration

- **Data Providers:**
  We explored how React Admin's data providers abstract the API layer, making it easy to connect to REST or GraphQL backends.
- **Error Handling, Caching, and Optimistic Updates:**
  By building robust error handling mechanisms, implementing caching strategies, and using optimistic updates, we ensured our dashboards remain responsive and reliable.
- **Real-Time Data Integration:**
  Whether through WebSockets or Server-Sent Events (SSE), we

learned how to bring real-time data into our dashboards, keeping users informed with live metrics.

Authentication and Authorization

- **Custom Authentication Providers:**
  We built custom auth providers to handle login, logout, and permission management.
- **Token Strategies and RBAC:**
  By understanding JWT, OAuth, and session-based strategies, and implementing Role-Based Access Control (RBAC), we ensured that our admin dashboards are secure and that access is controlled.

Personal Reflection:
Mastering these concepts transformed my approach to building admin interfaces. I learned that a robust architecture, thoughtful state management, and attention to performance and security are the cornerstones of professional React development. Each technique and tool we discussed is a piece of the puzzle, contributing to an efficient, scalable, and user-friendly application.

C 2: Future Trends in React Admin Development

The landscape of web development is constantly evolving, and so is React Admin. Staying ahead means understanding and adopting future trends that promise to make admin dashboards more powerful, efficient, and user-friendly. In this guide, we'll explore emerging trends in React Admin development, including server components and concurrent mode, advanced state management and data fetching strategies, headless CMS integration, and real-time analytics powered by AI and ML. We'll also provide practical examples and expert commentary to help you prepare for the future.

Personal Insight:
I've observed that as applications grow more complex and user expectations rise, the tools and patterns we use must evolve. Embracing future trends not only improves performance and usability but also opens

up new ways to deliver insights and interactivity. Let's dive into these trends and see how they can shape the next generation of admin dashboards.

---

1. Server Components and Concurrent Mode

Overview

React Server Components and **Concurrent Mode** are set to revolutionize how we build and render UIs. Server Components allow you to render parts of your application on the server, reducing bundle sizes and offloading computation from the client. Concurrent Mode lets React prepare multiple versions of the UI simultaneously, improving responsiveness.

Key Benefits

- **Reduced Bundle Sizes:**
  By rendering heavy components on the server, you reduce the JavaScript sent to the client.
- **Improved Performance:**
  Concurrent Mode can interrupt and prioritize renders, leading to smoother interactions.
- **Enhanced Scalability:**
  Offloading some rendering tasks to the server allows client devices to perform better, especially on mobile.

Practical Example: Enabling Concurrent Features

While full adoption is still experimental, you can start preparing your codebase. For instance, using React's experimental features:

```
// File: src/index.js
import React from 'react';
import ReactDOM from 'react-dom/client';
import App from './App';

// Experimental concurrent mode setup (available in React
18+)
```

```
const root =
ReactDOM.createRoot(document.getElementById('root'));
root.render(
  <React.StrictMode>
    <App />
  </React.StrictMode>
);
```

Expert Commentary:
Concurrent Mode is poised to change our approach to rendering. Although its full potential is still unfolding, early experiments indicate that it can drastically reduce latency and improve the user experience on complex dashboards.

---

2. Advanced State Management and Data Fetching

Overview

New state management libraries and data fetching strategies are emerging as alternatives to traditional Redux. Libraries like **Recoil** and **Zustand** offer a more granular and intuitive approach to global state management. At the same time, GraphQL is gaining traction as a more efficient alternative to REST, enabling more precise data queries.

Key Trends

- **Recoil:**
  Provides a minimal API with atoms and selectors, making it easier to manage shared state with fine-grained control.
- **Zustand:**
  Offers a simple, unopinionated way to manage state with a very small footprint.
- **GraphQL Integration:**
  Modern data providers for React Admin are beginning to incorporate GraphQL, enabling more efficient data retrieval and updates.

Practical Example: Using Recoil for Global State

1. **Install Recoil:**

```
npm install recoil
```

2. **Set Up a Recoil Atom and Selector:**

```javascript
// File: src/state/userState.js
import { atom, selector } from 'recoil';

export const userState = atom({
  key: 'userState',
  default: null,
});

export const isAuthenticatedSelector = selector({
  key: 'isAuthenticated',
  get: ({ get }) => !!get(userState),
});
```

3. **Use Recoil in Your App:**

```javascript
// File: src/App.js
import React from 'react';
import { RecoilRoot, useRecoilValue } from 'recoil';
import { isAuthenticatedSelector } from
'./state/userState';
import Dashboard from './components/Dashboard';

const AppContent = () => {
  const isAuthenticated =
useRecoilValue(isAuthenticatedSelector);
  return isAuthenticated ? <Dashboard /> : <div>Please log
in</div>;
};

const App = () => (
  <RecoilRoot>
    <AppContent />
  </RecoilRoot>
);

export default App;
```

Expert Commentary:
Switching to newer state management libraries like Recoil can simplify global state handling, especially in complex admin dashboards where

multiple components share state. These tools integrate smoothly with React and can reduce boilerplate while offering powerful features.

---

3. Headless CMS Integration

Overview

The rise of headless CMS platforms has transformed how content is managed and delivered. In a headless CMS setup, content is decoupled from presentation, allowing your React Admin dashboard to fetch data through APIs and display it dynamically.

Key Benefits

- **Flexibility:**
  Easily manage and update content across multiple platforms.
- **Scalability:**
  Decoupling content management from the front end makes it easier to scale.
- **Enhanced User Experience:**
  Real-time content updates and dynamic displays improve engagement.

Practical Implementation: Fetching Content from a Headless CMS

For example, using a headless CMS like Strapi:

```javascript
// File: src/dataProviderCMS.js
const cmsUrl = 'https://cms.example.com';

const cmsDataProvider = {
  getList: (resource, params) =>
    fetch(`${cmsUrl}/${resource}`, {
      method: 'GET',
    })
      .then((response) => response.json())
      .then((data) => ({ data: data.items, total:
data.total })),
  // Implement other CRUD methods as needed
};
```

```
export default cmsDataProvider;
```

Expert Commentary:
Headless CMS solutions enable dynamic, content-rich admin dashboards that can be updated in real time without redeploying your application. This trend is rapidly gaining momentum and is likely to shape the future of content management in admin interfaces.

4. Real-Time Analytics with AI and Machine Learning

Overview

The integration of AI and ML with real-time analytics is a forward-looking trend that promises to revolutionize how data is interpreted. By leveraging machine learning algorithms, dashboards can offer predictive insights, anomaly detection, and automated reporting.

Practical Example: Integrating a Real-Time Anomaly Detection API

Imagine an API that flags anomalies in system metrics. You can integrate it into your dashboard to highlight issues as they occur.

```
// File: src/components/AnomalyDashboard.js
import React, { useEffect, useState } from 'react';
import { ResponsiveContainer, LineChart, Line, XAxis,
YAxis, Tooltip, Legend } from 'recharts';

const AnomalyDashboard = () => {
  const [metrics, setMetrics] = useState([]);
  const [anomalies, setAnomalies] = useState([]);

  useEffect(() => {
    // Simulate fetching real-time data and anomaly
detection
    const interval = setInterval(() => {
      const newMetric = {
        time: new Date().toISOString(),
        value: Math.floor(Math.random() * 100),
```

```
      };
      setMetrics((prev) => [newMetric, ...prev].slice(0,
20));

      // Simulate anomaly detection logic
      if (newMetric.value > 80) {
        setAnomalies((prev) => [newMetric, ...prev]);
      }
    }, 5000);
    return () => clearInterval(interval);
  }, []);

  return (
    <div style={{ margin: '2rem auto', width: '90%' }}>
      <h2 style={{ textAlign: 'center' }}>Real-Time Metrics
with Anomaly Detection</h2>
      <ResponsiveContainer width="100%" height={300}>
        <LineChart data={metrics} margin={{ top: 20, right:
30, left: 20, bottom: 5 }}>
          <XAxis dataKey="time" tickFormatter={(time) =>
new Date(time).toLocaleTimeString()} />
          <YAxis />
          <Tooltip labelFormatter={(time) => new
Date(time).toLocaleTimeString()} />
          <Legend />
          <Line type="monotone" dataKey="value"
stroke="#8884d8" dot={{ r: 3 }} />
          {/* Highlight anomalies */}
          {anomalies.length > 0 && (
            <Line
              type="monotone"
              dataKey="value"
              data={anomalies}
              stroke="#ff0000"
              dot={{ r: 5 }}
              name="Anomalies"
            />
          )}
        </LineChart>
      </ResponsiveContainer>
    </div>
  );
};

export default AnomalyDashboard;
```

Explanation:

- **Real-Time Data Simulation:**
  New metrics are added every 5 seconds.
- **Anomaly Detection:**
  A simple condition flags high values as anomalies.
- **Dual-Line Chart:**
  The main line chart displays overall metrics, while anomalies are highlighted in red.

Expert Commentary:
Integrating AI and ML techniques into real-time dashboards opens up new avenues for proactive decision-making. Although this example is simplified, it illustrates the potential of merging real-time data visualization with predictive analytics.

Future trends in React Admin development are set to transform the way we build, scale, and interact with admin dashboards. Key areas of innovation include:

- **Server Components and Concurrent Mode:**
  Enhancing performance and responsiveness.
- **Advanced State Management and GraphQL Integration:**
  Enabling more efficient data flows.
- **Headless CMS and Real-Time Content:**
  Allowing for dynamic, scalable content management.
- **Real-Time Analytics with AI and ML:**
  Providing predictive insights and automated anomaly detection.

By staying ahead of these trends, you can build admin interfaces that are not only robust and efficient but also ready to adapt to the evolving demands of modern web applications.

Personal Reflection:
The future of React Admin is both exciting and challenging. Embracing these trends requires continuous learning and experimentation. I encourage you to explore these emerging technologies, experiment with new libraries, and always keep user experience and performance at the forefront.

C.3: Recommendations for Further Learning

Learning is a continuous journey, especially in a field as dynamic as web development. Here are some recommendations to help you deepen your understanding of React Admin and related technologies:

1. Official Documentation and Tutorials

- **React Official Docs:**
  React Documentation is an excellent resource for understanding the core principles of React.
- **React Admin Documentation:**
  The *React Admin Docs* provide comprehensive guides, API references, and tutorials.
- **Redux Documentation:**
  If you're working with Redux, the *Redux Docs* offer detailed explanations and best practices.

2. Courses

- **Online Courses:**
  - Courses on platforms like Udemy, Coursera, or Pluralsight that focus on advanced React and Redux concepts.
  - Specialized courses in data visualization and real-time web development can further enhance your skill set.

3. Community and Open Source

- **GitHub and Stack Overflow:**
  Engage with the community by contributing to open-source projects or asking questions on Stack Overflow. This practical exposure often provides insights that documentation cannot.
- **Meetups and Conferences:**
  Attend React and JavaScript meetups or conferences (either virtually or in person) to network with other developers and learn about the latest trends.

4. Experiment and Build

- **Side Projects:**
  Build your own admin dashboard or contribute to existing open-source projects. Experimenting with new features, such as real-time updates or advanced authentication, reinforces your learning.
- **Code Reviews:**
  Participate in code reviews or study well-architected open-source projects to understand different approaches to similar problems.

Personal Reflection:
Continuous learning has been one of the most rewarding parts of my career. Exploring new libraries, experimenting with emerging technologies, and engaging with the community have all contributed to my growth as a developer. I encourage you to stay curious and never stop learning.

As we conclude this journey through Professional React Admin Development, remember that each concept, technique, and tool we've discussed is a stepping stone towards building more powerful, efficient, and user-friendly applications. From setting up your environment to implementing complex state management, performance optimizations, and advanced API integrations, you now have a comprehensive toolkit at your disposal.

The future of React Admin is bright, with continuous advancements in performance, real-time data integration, and developer tooling. Embrace these changes, experiment boldly, and let your admin dashboards evolve to meet the needs of tomorrow.

Appendices

The appendices section serves as a comprehensive reference to support your continued growth and success in React Admin development. Here, you'll find essential resources, debugging and performance profiling tools, deployment strategies, frequently asked questions, and a glossary of key terms. These supplementary materials are designed to enhance your learning experience and serve as a quick reference guide as you build and maintain sophisticated admin dashboards.

A.1: Essential Resources and Documentation

Staying current with documentation and industry resources is crucial in the fast-paced world of web development. Below are some invaluable sources that can help you deepen your knowledge and solve problems effectively.

React Documentation

- **React Official Docs:**
  The official *React documentation* is the definitive resource for understanding React fundamentals, Hooks, and advanced patterns. It's continuously updated with the latest best practices.
- **React Blog and RFCs:**
  Explore the *React blog* and *RFCs* to stay informed about upcoming features and improvements.

React Admin Documentation

- **React Admin Docs:**
  The *React Admin documentation* provides extensive guides, API references, and examples specifically tailored to building admin interfaces. It's an essential resource for both beginners and experienced developers.

MDN Web Docs

- **MDN:**
  MDN Web Docs is a treasure trove of information on web standards including HTML, CSS, and JavaScript. It's particularly useful for understanding browser behavior and troubleshooting front-end issues.

GitHub Repositories

- **Open Source Projects:**
  Explore repositories on _GitHub_ related to React Admin. Studying open-source projects can offer insights into best practices, advanced techniques, and common challenges in real-world applications.
- **Community Contributions:**
  Engage with the community by reviewing issues, pull requests, and discussions. This not only aids in learning but also in contributing back to the ecosystem.

Personal Insight:
I've often found that the best solutions come from the collective knowledge available on GitHub and MDN. Don't hesitate to dive into these resources, experiment with sample projects, and contribute to discussions—the community is one of the strongest assets in our field.

A.2: Debugging Tools and Performance Profiling

Efficient debugging and performance profiling are crucial for maintaining a high-quality application. This section covers tools and strategies to help you identify, diagnose, and resolve issues quickly.

Debugging Tools

- **React DevTools:**
  React DevTools is an essential browser extension that allows you to inspect React component hierarchies, view props and state, and monitor re-renders.

- **Redux DevTools:**
  If you're using Redux, the _Redux DevTools_ extension provides a time-travel debugging feature, enabling you to track state changes and understand how actions impact your store.
- **Browser Developer Tools:**
  Modern browsers (Chrome, Firefox, Edge) come equipped with powerful developer tools for debugging JavaScript, inspecting network requests, and profiling performance.

Performance Profiling

- **Performance Tab (Chrome DevTools):**
  Use the Performance tab to record and analyze your application's runtime performance. It helps you identify bottlenecks in rendering and script execution.
- **Lighthouse:**
  Lighthouse is an open-source, automated tool for improving the quality of web pages. It offers insights on performance, accessibility, and best practices.
- **React Profiler:**
  The React Profiler tool within React DevTools can help you understand the performance of your React components by measuring render times and identifying unnecessary re-renders.

Personal Insight:
I often use a combination of React DevTools and Lighthouse when optimizing a project. Profiling can reveal unexpected performance issues, and the iterative process of debugging and profiling has been instrumental in building smooth, responsive applications.

A.3: Deployment Strategies and Best Practices

Deploying your React Admin application effectively is key to ensuring reliability, performance, and security in production. Here are some strategies and best practices:

Deployment Platforms

- **Vercel:**
  Offers seamless deployment for Next.js and static sites with a focus on speed and ease of use.
- **Netlify:**
  Provides continuous deployment, serverless functions, and a global CDN, making it a great choice for static and dynamic applications.
- **Heroku:**
  A platform-as-a-service (PaaS) that supports various backend languages and is excellent for deploying full-stack applications.
- **AWS Amplify / Firebase:**
  Ideal for scalable, serverless architectures with integrated backend services.

Best Practices

- **Build Optimization:**
  Use tools like Webpack and Babel to bundle and optimize your code. Create production builds using `npm run build` and ensure that code splitting and lazy loading are properly configured.
- **Environment Variables:**
  Manage configuration settings with environment variables, keeping sensitive data out of your source code.
- **Security Measures:**
  Ensure that your deployed application uses HTTPS, implements CORS policies, and follows best practices for secure API communication.
- **Monitoring and Logging:**
  Use monitoring tools like Sentry, New Relic, or LogRocket to track performance and catch runtime errors in production.
- **CI/CD Pipelines:**
  Automate your deployment process with continuous integration and continuous deployment (CI/CD) tools. This minimizes manual errors and speeds up updates.

Personal Insight:
I've found that a well-automated deployment process not only saves time but also significantly reduces downtime and errors in production. Platforms like Netlify and Vercel make it easy to roll out changes quickly and safely.

A.4: Frequently Asked Questions (FAQ)

A frequently asked questions (FAQ) section can be an invaluable resource for quickly resolving common issues and clarifying concepts. While this section is typically maintained separately, here are some common questions:

- **Q:** How do I optimize React Admin performance?
  - o **A:** Utilize code splitting, lazy loading, and virtualization techniques to reduce initial load times and minimize unnecessary re-renders.
- **Q:** What is the best way to manage global state in a React Admin application?
  - o **A:** Redux is a popular choice for complex state management, but alternatives like Recoil or Zustand might be suitable for smaller projects.
- **Q:** How can I secure my API endpoints?
  - o **A:** Implement token-based authentication (e.g., JWT), enforce HTTPS, use rate limiting, and validate inputs to secure your API.
- **Q:** Which charting library should I use?
  - o **A:** It depends on your needs. Chart.js and Recharts are great for standard visualizations, while D3.js offers unparalleled customization for complex charts.

Personal Insight:
Creating an FAQ section in your project documentation helps reduce repetitive queries and provides a quick reference for both new and experienced developers. It's a simple step that can dramatically improve developer efficiency.

A.5: Glossary of Terms

Understanding terminology is crucial for effective communication in development. Here's a brief glossary of key terms:

- **Admin Dashboard:** A web interface for managing and monitoring application data.

- **Authentication:** The process of verifying a user's identity.
- **Authorization:** The process of determining whether a user has permission to perform a certain action.
- **Data Provider:** An abstraction layer in React Admin that manages communication with the backend API.
- **JWT (JSON Web Token):** A compact, URL-safe means of representing claims to be transferred between two parties.
- **OAuth:** An authorization framework that enables applications to obtain limited access to user accounts on an HTTP service.
- **RBAC (Role-Based Access Control):** A method for regulating access to resources based on the roles of individual users.
- **Virtualization:** A technique for rendering only visible data to improve performance with large datasets.
- **Code Splitting:** The process of breaking down a codebase into smaller chunks that are loaded on demand.
- **Lazy Loading:** Loading components or modules only when they are needed.

Personal Insight:
A well-maintained glossary is an indispensable tool, especially when collaborating with others or revisiting a project after some time. It ensures that everyone is on the same page and that technical jargon doesn't become a barrier to understanding.

This appendices chapter is designed to be your go-to reference as you continue your journey in React Admin development. Whether you're debugging, deploying, or simply need a quick lookup for key terms, these resources, tools, and best practices will serve you well.

Personal Reflection:
Throughout my own journey, I found that having clear, well-organized supplementary materials greatly accelerated my learning and development process. I encourage you to refer back to these appendices regularly as you encounter new challenges and opportunities in your projects.

Happy coding, and may these resources empower you to build robust, efficient, and innovative admin dashboards!